THE D-DAY LANDINGS
AND THE BATTLE OF NORMANDY

Pour Julien,

Mon petit-fils que j'adore
à l'occasion de son 8ème anniversaire.
En espérant que tu trouveras beaucoup
d'inspiration dans le courage de tous ces
jeunes soldats.

Je t'embrasse très fort,

Manou

July 2004.

THE D-DAY LANDINGS

AND THE BATTLE OF NORMANDY

JEAN-BERNARD MOREAU

Doctor of History

Head of the Memorial History Department

Translation : John Ritchie

Le Mémorial de Caen

UN MUSÉE POUR LA PAIX

Contents

From Dunkirk to the Normandy beaches...

May 1940. After invading Luxembourg, the Netherlands and Belgium, the German armies had entered France. The British, who had come to support the French army in its fight against the *Wehrmacht*, were surrounded not far from Dunkirk. Driven back onto the neighbouring beaches, they re-embarked in desperation, thus saving most of the expeditionary force sent to France.

Four years later, almost to the day, and after some failed attempts and much discussion, Her Majesty's troops set foot on the continent once again, as Winston Churchill had promised in July 1940, when he had declared that they would be back as soon as the necessary men and equipment were ready. But the British who landed in Normandy this time had not come back to France alone. They were part of the great coalition of Nazi Germany's declared enemies, built up over the intervening years and resulting from many conferences between the allies.

The landing on the 6th of June 1944, rightly considered to be one of the decisive phases of the Second World War, was as much the result of lengthy technical preparations as that of negotiations between dispassionate allies, who sometimes disagreed on strategy.

The Normandy landings: a decision wrought from conference to conference

As of 1940, Churchill decided to create commando units whose task it was to organise raids on the occupying German forces in Europe. During October, while London was being bombed by the *Luftwaffe,* the British Prime Minister asked his army commanders to study the possibility of launching offensive operations on the continent and, particularly, to consider the idea of landing on the north-west coast of France. He then turned to the United States for help, America alone having the industrial potential necessary to fulfil his ambitions.

Thus, three Anglo-American conferences took place in 1941, the first from January to March, in Washington, the second in August, in mid-Atlantic, on board the *Prince of Wales,* and the third back in the American capital in December. During the first two meetings, and because the American leadership was maintaining a very strongly isolationist diplomatic stance, the principles of joint action against Germany were the main subject of discussion. But, in December, the Japanese surprise attack on Pearl Harbour and the German declaration of war on the United States brought those same leaders to reconsider and renounce their hitherto held non-interventionist position. At the same time as President Roosevelt was preparing the American riposte against Japan, he ordered action against Hitler's Reich, whose political orientation he considered prejudicial for American interests worldwide. This campaign was jointly conceived and undertaken with the British.

One immediate result of this spectacular reinforcement of the links between the two Anglo-Saxon powers was the creation, in early 1942, of a general staff for joint aero-nautical and terrestrial operations, but the American president grew impatient with the slow pace of its development. So, in April, General Marshall put forward a plan for an invasion of Europe to happen the following spring. This plan provided for the establishment of a bridgehead in France, between the estuaries of the Seine and the Somme. Roosevelt approved the project, and the commander of the US Army's general staff travelled to London to present it to the British leaders, who did not oppose the undertaking, although they were rather reticent. The first phase of the plan was launched in May. Code-named 'Bolero', the project consisted in transporting a million men and necessary equipment to Great Britain. Although the operation began straight away, the transfer was not to be completed until two years later. Between times, the American project was the subject of much dissension, and was substantially modified.

The Normandy landings: a source of disagreement between the powers in coalition against Germany

June 1942. Whereas the Soviet leadership, confronted with the accumulated defeats of the Red Army at the hands of the *Wehrmacht* on the eastern front, was insisting on the launching of a second, western front, Churchill expressed doubts about making an invasion on the coast of north-western Europe a priority. The British Prime Minister agreed that such an operation would be a decisive event in the course of the war, but he was of the opinion that the Allies could only hope to emerge victorious from the confrontation on the condition that the Germans be obliged to disperse their forces in different areas of operation beforehand, notably in the Mediterranean. So, contrary to the opinion of the American President, who was under pressure from the Soviets, and who had adopted the idea of sending troops into the heart of Germany as rapidly as possible, the head of the British government refused the strategy of a direct attack in the Channel.

However, and although he was dealing with the urgent and repeated requests from Admiral King, commander of the US Navy in the Pacific, for reinforcements to combat the Japanese, Roosevelt finally gave satisfaction to Churchill, who made no secret of his mistrust of the Soviets. At the end of 1942, the Americans and the British agreed to slow down operation 'Bolero' and prepare operation 'Torch', whose aim was to disembark allied troops in French North Africa. Eisenhower, who was entrusted with the supreme command of the expeditionary forces, brought this operation, dreamt up during the summer, to a rapid and successful conclusion. On the 8th of November almost 75,000 men landed on the beaches of Casablanca, Algiers, and Oran; on the 10th, the Anglo-American forces were in control of Morocco and Algeria, after forty-eight hours of fighting of varying intensity, depending on the sector.

Shortly after the success of operation Torch, Churchill and Roosevelt met in Casablanca in January 1943. The two men, accompanied by their chiefs of staff and military advisors, set about ironing out their strategic divergences. From the outset, the British point of view prevailed once again: the liberation of North Africa should be used as a springboard for an invasion of Sicily which, were it to be undertaken in July of that same year, would signal the start of the re-conquest of occupied Europe. However, in the case of failure or if the results proved insufficiently conclusive, a large-scale operation would be launched from England.

This projection was adopted, as the scenario seemed far from improbable, and a strategic research department came into being forthwith. This department was given the task of producing a blueprint for the offensive. It was set up in London in April, and the chief of the British 1st Army was put in charge. During the nomination process of the Supreme Commander of the forces being brought together, General Sir Frederick Morgan carried out the functions of the Chief of Staff to Supreme Allied Commander, or COSSAC, an acronym which quickly came to designate the whole army staff, and not just its director.

Where to invade, and how?

These were the questions which Cossac's strategists had to answer. Of the two questions, however, it was that of location to which they first turned their attentions. Indeed, the idea of landing on the French shores meant attacking the Atlantikwall, a complex system of defences along the whole of the western European coast, which the Germans had started building back in December 1941. On the Allied side, and in spite of the experience gained during the landings previously organised, the memory of the resounding defeat suffered during operation Jubilee on the 19th of August 1942 was uppermost in everyone's mind; that day, the raid by Anglo-Canadian troops on Dieppe, designed to test the German defences on the French coast, had ended in disaster. Half the 6,000-strong force had been killed, wounded or captured; the others had fled.

So it is not surprising that Cossac did not pursue the option of landing in the Pas-de-Calais, at the northern tip of France. The coast there, the closest to England, presented many advantages: proximity to German territory, maximal possibilities for air support and the rapid turn-around of supply ships, and numerous existing ports. The Germans, who were also conscious that the zone was propitious for an offensive, had preventively reinforced the density of their coastal defences there: the many fortified positions and the massive presence of men and tanks rapidly dissuaded the Allied military chiefs from considering the region.

With these factors taken into account, the area finally settled on was the Seine Bay area. Situated between the Orne and Vire estuaries, the beaches there were less heavily fortified. Moreover, this part of the Normandy coastline had the added advantage of being easy to isolate from the rest of France, by bombarding bridges on the Seine and the Loire. The destruction of these bridges would make the influx of enemy reinforcements more difficult, and give the Allies more time to land reinforcements.

The Cossac project favoured the rapid launch of a front spread along a forty-kilometre section of the coast and recommended attacking three beaches, which were ascribed the code names *Omaha, Gold* and *Juno* for the occasion. Each of them was to be besieged by an infantry division transported by sea, the landing troops having been preceded by two airborne divisions. To compensate for the lack of port facilities in the sector, fresh supplies for the troops would be provided by means of an artificial port, which would be constructed offshore from the attack zone, as soon as positions on the shore had been consolidated.

All the Allied chiefs of staff accepted the Cossac propositions during a meeting in Quebec in August 1943, and confirmed in November of that year by Roosevelt, Churchill and Stalin in Teheran at the first of their tri-partite conferences. In December, with the nomination of General Eisenhower to the post of supreme commander of the Allied armies in Europe, the operations previously planned in the Mediterranean were shelved in favour of operation *Overlord*.

Waiting for D-Day

1

Left-hand page: Britain. Allied troops in training, somewhere on the Devon coast.

Below: Normandy coast. On the other side of the Channel, a German sentinel in position on one section of the Atlantic Wall.

In Britain, the Allies were actively preparing the different operational aspects of a future landing on the north-west coast of Europe.

On the other side of the Channel, the Germans applied themselves to the reinforcement of their system of coastal defences, behind which they had taken up position months before, in the run-up to the events they knew to be inevitable, but not knowing when nor where they would happen.

1. In Britain: preparations for an unprecedented and unparalleled invasion

Bushey Park, Headquarters of the SHAEF, 12th February 1944. The Allied Staff around General Dwight D. Eisenhower, Commander-in-Chief of the Allied forces. From left to right: General O. Bradley, Commander of the 1st US Army, Admiral B. Ramsay, Commander of the Naval Forces; Air Marshall A. Tedder, Deputy Commander-in-Chief; General Eisenhower; General B. Montgomery, Field-Marshal; Air Marshal T. Leigh Mallory, Commander of the Air Forces; General W. Bedell-Smith, Head of the Commander-in-Chief's Allied Staff.

The moment General Eisenhower arrived in Britain, on the 14th of January 1944, he set up SHAEF, *Supreme Headquarters Allied Expeditionary Force,* or in other words, the great general headquarters of the Allied expeditionary force incorporating Cossac's departments. The commander-in-chief of the Allied forces in Europe set up in a vast camp near London, at Bushey Park, and surrounded himself with a team of experienced men who were known above all for their hardened character, and whose reputation preceded them.

The choice of SHAEF

Eisenhower chose a British aviator as his deputy, Air Marshal Arthur Tedder, commander of the Allied air forces in the Mediterranean, and designated a compatriot he knew well, General Walter Bedell-Smith, to be his Chief of Staff. As commander of the naval forces, he appointed Admiral Bertram H. Ramsay, who had overseen the evacuation from Dunkirk in 1940, and the Allied landing in French North Africa in November 1942. Command of the combined air forces was entrusted to Air Marshal Trafford Leigh-Mallory, a battle of Britain veteran who had also participated in the raid on Dieppe in August 1942. Finally, he gave command of the terrestrial army to General Bernard L. Montgomery, who had triumphed over Field-marshal Rommel at El-Alamein. Montgomery, being commander in chief of the Allied 21st Army group and, consequently, commander of the D-Day offensive on the beaches, had authority over the American 1st Army and the British 2nd Army, respectively commanded by the Generals Bradley and Dempsey.

Once recruited, this team took up the task begun by the Cossac, yet without modifying any of the collective choices made under General Morgan's stewardship. The choice of the Seine Bay area as landing site was never called into question, but the initial version of operation Overlord was modified, sometimes substantially; the main change in the plan concerned the size of the assault sector, which Montgomery judged to be too restrictive, and which was revised at his request.

In order to strengthen the assault and to allow the first wave of troops to repel the enemy's counter-offensives, the terrestrial forces' commander considered it essential to compel the Germans to spread out their forces. With this in mind, he suggested adding an extra landing beach on each side of those already chosen. Furthermore, he recommended sending a second airborne division to the Cotentin to ensure the rapid capture of Cherbourg and its port. In his opinion, eight divisions should be involved from the first day of the assault: three airborne, five seaborne. Five more divisions would have to be transported by sea over the following two days.

The revised scale of operation Overlord constrained Eisenhower to devote more resources to it, and so its launch, initially planned for early May, was postponed for a month, particularly as there were insufficient boats available. However, at the beginning of April, the commander-in-chief of the Allied forces gave the order for Normandy to be isolated: the methodical bombardment of the north-west quarter of France began. This strategy was designed to limit the Germans' ability to bring reinforcements to the landing zone and to neutralise the radar stations spying on the Allies' movements in the air and on the sea.

The British and American Air Forces played a major role in the success of Overlord. During the ten weeks preceding the landing, the RAF and the US Air Force made some 200,000 sorties over the north-western quarter of France, during which 195,000 tonnes of bombs were dropped. The main road and rail communication hubs and most of the 92 enemy radar stations on the coast were destroyed: on D-Day, only 18 of them were still working.

In the night from 5th to 6th June, a party of airborne troops were transported on board British Horsa gliders, similar to those lined up here between two rows of Halifax bombers, which towed them.

Boats of all makes and sizes were anchored in all the ports on the south coast of England. In Southampton, the luxury cruise liners which lined the quays before the war, were replaced by the LCTs (Landing Craft – Tank), landing barges capable of setting down four to six 40-tonne tanks on the shore, and LCIs (Landing Craft – Infantry), capable of carrying 188 armed men or 75 tonnes of cargo. Battleships occupied the channel.

The amassing of resources and obsessive discretion

While the different departments of the SHAEF were putting the finishing touches to the invasion plan and preparing the terrain, the massive influx of American equipment finished the job of transforming England into a gigantic arsenal. In May 1944, almost 16,000 aeroplanes of all types, including 3,500 gliders, were lined up on aerodromes of all sizes, which were so numerous that a popular joke at the time suggested that it was possible to cross the country from north to south and from east to west without taking off, just following the runways. The ports were jammed with over 5,000 warships, combat ships and landing craft, not including the 1,600 merchant ships that were moored alongside them. In the fields, tens of thousands of tanks, armoured vehicles, lorries and jeeps were lined up row upon row, and hundreds of thousands of tonnes of arms and munitions were stockpiled in depots or out in the open.

Among the armoured vehicles were the «funnies», so-called because of their strange appearance. Scheduled to accompany the first wave of assault, whether it be with combat troops or engineers, these weird contraptions, mostly tanks, were specially designed to avoid the traps that had been invented by the Germans as part of their coastal defences. Under the command of General Hobart, a proven tank specialist, the British 79th Armoured Division was given the task of developing these machines in the spring of 1943. The men of this unit quickly proved themselves possessed of astonishing ingenuity, perfecting a whole series of specialised equipment which, when mounted on *Sherman* and *Churchill* tanks, endowed them with extra capabilities, without depriving them of their combat potential.

During the process of this extraordinary stockpiling of material, an equally impressive rallying of soldiers, seamen and airmen was under way. In May, over 3 million men had been mustered in England, ready to take part in the most massive amphibious operation ever undertaken. Beside the 1.7 million British troops were 1.5 million Americans, 200,000 Australians, Canadians and New-Zealanders, accompanied by 70,000 men of other nationalities. These others, citizens of countries occupied by the Germans, were French, (40,000), Polish (18,000), Belgian, Dutch, Norwegian, Danish, Czech and Greek. In total the Allied terrestrial army alone numbered 39 divisions, including General Leclerc's French 2nd Armoured Division and the Polish 1st Armoured Division led by General Maczek.

Having already become an arsenal, the south of England slowly flourished into a vast military camp. A rallying of this magnitude

American destroyers waiting for D-Day in one of the numerous British ports requisitioned for the occasion.

Tens of thousands of tanks, guns, and vehicles of all sorts were parked in serried ranks. Combat vehicles were to be found side by side with ambulances in these immense and unusual parking lots, which gradually filled up over the passing weeks.

caused a variety of problems, in particular with regard to accommodating the men. In order to cope with this need hotels, boarding houses, and schools were requisitioned, along with thousands of hectares of land on which canvas camps were pitched and Nissen huts (half-cylinders covered with corrugated iron) erected. But the main concern of the military chiefs was maintaining the utmost secrecy concerning where and how the invasion was to take place.

The coastal zones used as training grounds were quickly declared military areas and cleared of civilian residents. Among the 7,000 men of the SHAEF, only a handful had unrestricted access to all the information concerning the preparations for the invasion. The number of those in the know was strictly limited, to ensure maximum confidentiality.

But, as D-Day drew nearer, an ever-increasing number of officers received ever more detailed information about the missions on which they would be sent with their men. Little by little, the fear of careless, wagging tongues became an obsession with the chiefs of staff. At Eisenhower's behest, the usual security measures were applied with the utmost rigour: only strictly necessary contact with the outside was permitted; careless mistakes, absent-mindedness and talking too much were severely reprimanded. One note recommended that «no man should have access to letter boxes nor civilian telephones» and a pamphlet entitled «Dos and Don'ts...» was distributed to all units.

The Willys jeep, of which over 600,000 models were produced, was widely used by the Allied armies. It was designed in 1941, and was at first armed with a machine gun to be used as a reconnaissance vehicle. Afterwards used as a liaison or command vehicle, it also served as ambulance and pulled light anti-tank guns. The GIs said of it that you could 'ask it to do anything except cook!'.
Its characteristics and qualities – it was small and light, robust, manoeuvrable and fast – rapidly made it indispensable to the infantry, whose mobility it enhanced considerably.

Unable to count on finding supplies in France, which had been occupied and bled dry by the enemy, the Allied armies had to take everything they needed for the first days of the campaign, notably fuel. Seventeen million jerry cans were transported to Normandy.

Bridge-carrying tank. The installation of a «folding bridge», which was fixed to the bodywork of the tank, sometimes without its turret, allowed the landed vehicles to cross anti-tank trenches and small watercourses rapidly.

Crab flail tank. This tank was equipped with a rotating drum to which long metal chains were attached. It was designed to explode mines by lashing the ground in front as it moved forward.

Fascine tank. This tank, equipped with a huge bundle of wood, crossed anti-tank ditches without great difficulty.

Bobbin tank. This tank had a front-mounted drum, which laid down a wire netting path on the sand to ease the progress of other landed vehicles over sand and dune.

GENERAL HOBART'S « FUNNIES »

As did the soldiers of the other Allied units, those of the British 6th Airborne – here with General Richard Gale, who landed with them on the 6th of June – were regularly informed of the missions awaiting them. Orders to remain vigilant and on one's guard outside the camps were often repeated.

«DOS AND DON'TS

Remember that the enemy needs information and is prepared to do anything to get it. Remember that information is obtained by putting lots of scraps of information together, like a jigsaw.

Remember that any small indiscretion on your part might cost you not only your life, but also the lives of thousands of your comrades, and jeopardise the success of the whole military operation.

Do not reveal the name of the port where you will embark, nor the name of your boat, nor the date, nor the time of your departure, nor your itinerary.

Do not give any information to anybody, even to your family or to your friends. Do you think they will keep a secret that even you have been unable to?

Do not allow yourself to be stupidly provoked by a friend in order to prove that you know more than he does. He is perhaps less stupid than he may appear. Do not consume alcohol if you are incapable of discretion when drunk.

Do not try to send coded messages. The enemy is capable of decoding messages you send to your girlfriend back home.

FINALLY

Do not believe that because you have heard someone reveal secrets that you can do the same. Two blacks do not make a white.»

Pamphlet distributed to Allied soldiers stationed in England

Before embarking, the allied soldiers received a
brochure about France, in which figured the country's
customs, a few words and everyday expressions, and
the meaning of road signs.

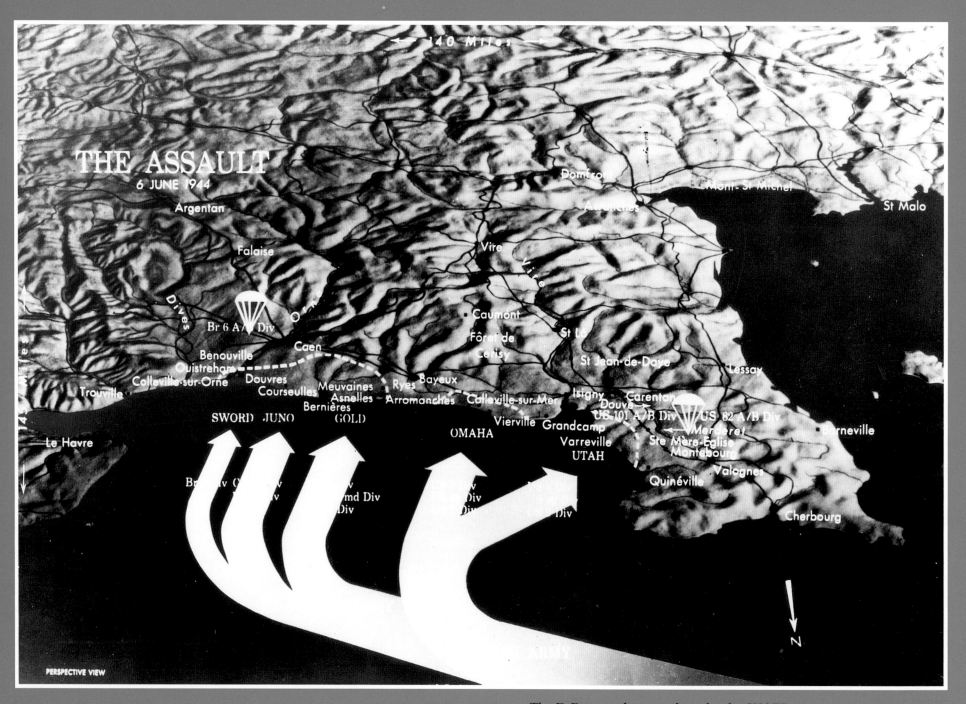

The D-Day assault mapped out by the SHAEF.

Innovations and objectives of operation Overlord

It was only in mid May that Eisenhower unveiled the definitive invasion plan to the Allied army commanders, assembled in an amphitheatre of St. Paul's School in London, with Winston Churchill and King George VI in attendance.

Contrary to the previous landings in the Mediterranean, which had taken place at high tide and at night, the Normandy landings were to happen at dawn, at mid-tide. This was, firstly, to allow the boats to avoid the various obstacles that the Germans had arranged along the beaches, which had been identified during the many reconnaissance flights undertaken by Allied pilots; and secondly to ensure that the preliminary aerial and marine bombardment resulted in an optimal reduction of the German coastal defences.

So, the day before D-Day, on the 5th of June, two fleets set sail: one, American, in the direction of the operation's two western sector sites, and the other, British, in the direction of the other three sites, towards the east. During the night, as the ships were approaching the coast, three airborne divisions were flown over the Normandy hinterland, to protect the flanks of the landing zone: two American divisions in the Cotentin and one British division to the east, between the river Orne and the river Dives. At dawn on D-Day, five infantry divisions – two American, two British and one Canadian – landed on the five beaches code-named *Utah, Omaha, Gold, Juno* and *Sword* respectively, transforming each of them into a bridgehead. The units that had been transported by boat were to link up and make contact with those transported by plane.

According to the plan, the troops were to take control of the terrain between the Orne estuary and the dunes on the beaches at Sainte-Marie-du-Mont in the Cotentin, as well as the towns of Caen and Bayeux, or in other words a coastal area approximately 100 km long and 17 km wide.

Finally, to ensure the replenishment of supplies and the sending of reinforcements for the troops already engaged in fighting, the construction of not only one but two artificial ports was planned, to be used until the capture of the port of Cherbourg. One was to be in the American sector, off *Omaha Beach* at Saint-Laurent; the other, in the British sector, off *Gold Beach*, at Arromanches.

In a dock in England, the construction of some of the 150 Phoenix hollow blocks which were to serve as the breakwaters for the artificial ports off Omaha and Gold beaches. They were 60 m long and 15 m wide, and the largest (around sixty) were 18 m high and weighed 6,044 tonnes.
The magnitude of these shipyard sites was such that it was practically impossible to hide them from any Luftwaffe reconnaissance aircraft that dared fly over the English coast. However, the German secret services never guessed what these hollow blocks would be used for. Even better, the secret of this gigantic task was so well kept, that most of the 20,000 workers and technicians requisitioned for 7 months to complete the work did not know what the blocks were to be used for either.

Fortitude, keeping the enemy in the dark

In the hope of increasing their chances of success, the Allied military commanders dreamt up the scheme of fooling the enemy by diverting their attention from the beaches of the Seine Bay. Code-named Fortitude, a double campaign of misinformation intended for the German high command was organised in parallel with the preparations for the landing in Normandy. One, Fortitude-North, aimed at giving the Germans reason to believe that the Allies intended attacking Norway and the other, Fortitude-South, the Dover Strait and the Pas-de-Calais.

To this purpose, the Anglo-Americans chased the German submarines patrolling off the Norwegian coast, bombarded the coastal defences between Dieppe and Dunkirk, and built ports, aerodromes and military equipment parks in the north-east of England. These were, however, of a very different quality to those existing in the south of the country. Although the number of vehicles stocked there was equivalent, the vehicles themselves were out of order, or simply fakes: in these parks, equipment declared unfit for use waited beside landing craft, planes or anti-tank guns made of plywood, beside rubber tanks and lorries.

For this gigantic red herring to be even more believable, an intense barrage of radio communication was maintained between fictitious command posts, and General Patton, who the Germans considered to be the most gifted of the Allied commanders in the art of tank warfare, was appointed commander of this phantom army group. Finally, and so as not to awaken suspicions in the enemy camp, where the slightest hint of trickery could have resulted in a redeployment of their troops, the destruction of the bridges over the Loire and the main communication nodes around Normandy was postponed until the day of the landings.

All things considered, operation Fortitude was a complete success. The German high command expected an Allied invasion more or less in the Pas-de-Calais, or perhaps on one side or the other of the Somme estuary. In spite of indications in reports brought back by the few of the *Luftwaffe's* reconnaissance flights to return from over the south-west of England, Marshal von Rundstedt, commander of the German forces on the western front, persisted in his belief, in May 1944, that the most threatened sector was still the shore between Le Havre and Calais. Even the arrival of Allied troops in Normandy in the first days of June did not change his conviction: following the example of the highest German authorities, he continued to wait for the real invasion.

Rubber tanks and lorries, plywood anti-tank guns and vehicles: just a few examples of the decoys gathered in the north-east of Great Britain as part of Operation Fortitude. This operation was directed by set designers from the theatrical world.
This red herring campaign was continued until the night of the 5th to 6th June, during which canvas dummies filled with a sand and straw mixture and equipped with a parachute were dropped around Rouen, Caen, and Saint-Lô, to increase the enemy's uncertainty and the confusion. Some of them were filled with small charges and delayed-action fuses, and imitated the noise of firing.

2. On the other side of the Channel: the Germans' nervous wait

The laying of tetrahedrons made from welded rails.

An invasion via the European coast over the Channel from England meant first of all succeeding in penetrating the Atlantikwall, the Germans' complex defensive system that they had started building in 1942. Hitler had been worried that the Allies might profit from the setbacks that the *Wehrmacht* was experiencing in the USSR to launch an offensive on the western front, and had decided to reinforce coastal defence systems back in December 1941.

The Atlantikwall, intended to foil a more than probable invasion

On the basis of the principle that this type of operation could not succeed without the control of a major port, Hitler ordered that «fortified sections and operational bases (be) established in such a manner as to be able to resist for a prolonged period, even when faced with superior enemy forces» all along the coasts from Norway to the Spanish border.

The attempted landing at Dieppe organised in August 1942 had confirmed the Führer's opinion that the Allies intended re-establishing their presence on the continent via the north western seaboard. That attempt had also gone some way to comforting him in his strategic choice: the construction of a string of fortifications would allow an infantry battalion, even a mediocre one, to inflict heavy losses on assailants. In his opinion Dieppe's unfinished defences, which had succeeded in halting 6,000 Anglo-Canadians, were proof of this. Moreover, these fortifications alone demonstrated the validity of the Atlantic Wall.

After two years of work, some 15,000 fortifications lined the west coast of Europe. Over a million tonnes of steel, eleven million tonnes of concrete and 450,000 workers had been needed by the Todt organisation for the purposes of creating a defensive system similar to that of the Maginot line, parts of which had been salvaged and used on the Atlantic coasts. Some constructions resembled impregnable fortresses, with walls over 2 metres thick and armoured ceilings capable of withstanding high explosive shelling, but there were many others, which were more modest and were sometimes left unfinished.

So, at the beginning of 1944, far from being the insurmountable rampart that Hitler had wished for, the Atlantic Wall was even less effective as a «scarecrow» than the newspapers and the occupier-controlled cinema newsreels would have had people believe. Both, relaying German propaganda, boasted the merits and proclaimed the invulnerability of a defensive system that they presented as being unique in the world.

On site however, the reality was somewhat less advantageous. Whereas the port installations, submarine bases and the main strategic sectors were apparently capable of resisting powerful attacks, the rest of the coast showed signs of weaknesses at many points, defended as it was by rather thinly spread concrete operational bases, notably in the Seine Bay area. Thus, over the 1,400-odd kilometres of coastline between the Loire estuary and the Netherlands' dykes, there were at least 9,300 fortified buildings, but they were very unevenly spread, quantitatively and also qualitatively. There was one of these fortifications every 1,200 metres along the coast of the Calvados department, compared with a spacing of 750 metres to the North of Le Havre; there were three times fewer forts in Calvados than between the Seine estuary and the Pas-de-Calais.

Not only were they less numerous, but also more vulnerable and less well equipped. The anti-tank guns were left out in the open, as they had not yet had shelters built to house them; the same was true for the majority of the anti-aircraft guns and half of the big coastal guns, of which scarcely any were adequately powerful to challenge ships firing from out at sea. In the case of night-time operations, the use of powerful searchlights was supposed to make up for the lack of radar equipment.

The Atlantic Wall construction programme was entrusted to the Todt
Organisation, which worked on the Wall until the day before the landings. This
organisation, which bore the name of its founder, Dr. Fritz Todt, to whom Hitler
had entrusted the construction of the Siegfried Line, was attached to the
Wehrmacht in 1938.
As the war progressed, the workforce it employed, which was at first mainly
German, underwent a dramatic evolution. The German workers, who were quickly
mobilised in the army or industry, were replaced by foreign workers, of which
many were requisitioned in occupied territories. From 1941 onwards, barely 20%
of the Todt Organisation was German. These remaining Germans were principally
occupied with executive functions or overseeing work.

The Atlantic Wall workers were watched closely, and worked ceaselessly in difficult conditions, sometimes working night and day.

While the threat of an Allied landing became clearer, the *Wehrmacht* suffered setback upon setback on the Russian front. To slow the advancing Red Army, Hitler sent an ever-increasing number of divisions. Amongst them were the best of those who had up until then been posted on the western front, excepting those stationed to the north of the Seine estuary. Thus, from 1943 on, the units defending the coast were generally speaking relatively mediocre.

Being equipped with rather miscellaneous armaments, most of them were made up of reservists with little military training, whose age or handicaps debarred them from being sent to fight on the Russian front. Furthermore, certain infantry divisions were partially composed of whole battalions of «Eastern volunteers», a generic terms used to designate men from varying backgrounds, with varying motives for fighting in a German uniform. Beside genuine volunteers, who had joined up through ideology or opportunism, there were Soviet ex-prisoners of war recruited in *oflags* and *stalags,* who had preferred to wait for the end of the war this way rather than rot away in prison camps, where they were treated similarly to those interred in concentration camps.

Veritable entrenched camps on the edge of the shore, these concrete shelters protected the artillery from enemy bombardments, but they had the disadvantage of reducing the firing angle of the guns housed inside.

The smaller artillery batteries were responsible for the short-range defence of the shore. In Normandy, most of the anti-aircraft batteries and half of the coastal guns were of small or medium calibre. They were, in general, set up without shelter, right next to the beaches, as they were also intended to serve to prevent an offensive launched by landed troops.

The Germans used camouflage to make up for the small number of Luftwaffe units on the Western Front. In the seaside towns, houses were destroyed to make way for reinforced pillboxes, whose painted trompe l'oeil facades gave them the air of peaceful holiday villas.
Along the beaches and the cliffs, concrete shelters were covered with natural vegetation, or hidden under nets.

Between 1941 and 1945, over one million citizens of the different Soviet Republics volunteered for service in the Wehrmacht. The Russians, Ukrainians, Cossacks, Armenians, Azerbaijanis, Georgians, Northern Caucasians, Turkistanis and Tartars from the Volga region, who all had different reasons for having joined the German army, and who wore its uniform, were termed «Eastern Volunteers».

THE «EASTERN VOLUNTEERS»

At the beginning of 1944, 75,000 of them were sent to France, in 75 battalions. Over half of them were made available to the OB West under Marshal von Rundstedt. Divisions of these men, consisting of two or three battalions, were incorporated into infantry regiments, which were as often as not charged with the defence of the Atlantikwall. In June 1944, the German 7th Army numbered 23 such battalions, of which eight were stationed in the Cotentin, and another four were on the Calvados coast.

Above: a moment of relaxation for these Russian volunteers, whose battalion was stationed on the coast near Coutances, in the Cotentin.

Centre: papers printed in their own language were distributed to these volunteers, as many of them spoke no German.

Bottom: Turkmenistani volunteers, whose battalion was part of the German 711th Infantry, praying under the guidance of two mullahs near Deauville.

Thus, on Omaha, Gold and Sword beaches, Ukrainians were amongst the forces that would attempt to repel the Allied invasion. In the Cotentin, Georgians of the 795th Battalion of Eastern Volunteers, part of the German 709th Division, participated in the combat around Sainte-Mère-Église. Following the loss of that position, the survivors joined the ranks of Colonel van der Heydte's 6th Parachute Regiment, to oppose the American entry into Carentan.

Turkmenistanis incorporated into the German 270th Infantry stationed near Cherbourg, where they received training in coastal defence.

The *Panzerkontroverse,*
or Rundstedt-Rommel disagreement

Within the *Wehrmacht,* many officers were wary of the static defences; notable among them was Field-marshal von Rundstedt who Hitler had appointed commander-in-chief of the western front in March 1942. Although he was conscious that the Germans' defensive system was far from impregnable, he nevertheless fed the propaganda that shored up the *Atlantikwall.* In February 1944, he attempted pulling the wool over the eyes of the watching world, declaring that «the enemy will come up against a coastal system of a very different scale from those that he has encountered to date. [...] The fortified coastal positions are very much more effective and are capable of resisting bombardments.» However, in private, he made no secret of his scepticism with regard to the system's effectiveness, which he reckoned just capable of temporarily delaying an Allied offensive, but not of stopping one. It was in his words, «a monumental bluff, designed more to fool the German people than the enemy.»

He was in favour of mobile warfare, and recommended relying on armoured divisions stationed far inland and kept systematically at maximum readiness. In to his view, only this kind of unit, used to counter-attack massively and forcefully, would make it possible to victoriously succeed in repelling assailants, who would be particularly vulnerable just after having landed and as they awaited reinforcements and moved inland.

Field-marshal Rommel shared his superior's misgivings regarding the declared effectiveness of the Atlantic wall, but not his opinions concerning the use of armoured divisions. Rommel had been commander of the terrestrial forces on the western front since March 1943 and was responsible for ensuring the defence of a front reaching from Belgium to the Loire estuary in this capacity. He declared that *«the war will be won or lost on the beaches»* and that *«the first twenty four hours of the invasion will prove decisive [...] for the Allies, as it will be for Germany, this will be the war's longest day.»*

Wishing armoured divisions to be stationed very close to the coast to allow them to intervene without delay, the *Wehrmacht's* youngest field-marshal, who agreed with Hitler that the Allies must be repelled from the moment they landed on the beaches, advocated the reinforcement of the coastal defences. Thus being considered a partisan of defence by Hitler, Rommel was appointed inspector general of the North Sea and Atlantic fortifications in November 1943.

In March 1942, Marshal von Rundstedt (centre) was given the difficult task of defending 5,000 km of coastline. He was 67 years old, and it was said that he was disillusioned. However, and despite incurring Hitler's displeasure, he continued to criticise his strategic choices openly, notably concerning the defence of the Western Front, on which subject he was opposed to Marshal Rommel (left, facing General Gause, his chief of staff until March 1944).
Hitler, the supreme arbiter of the disagreement between the two Marshals, decided on a compromise solution: half of the armoured divisions would be stationed near the coast, the others would be kept inland.

The setting of stakes in the beaches, which was at first a lengthy and tiresome task, was accelerated and facilitated by the use of fire hoses to dig up the sand.

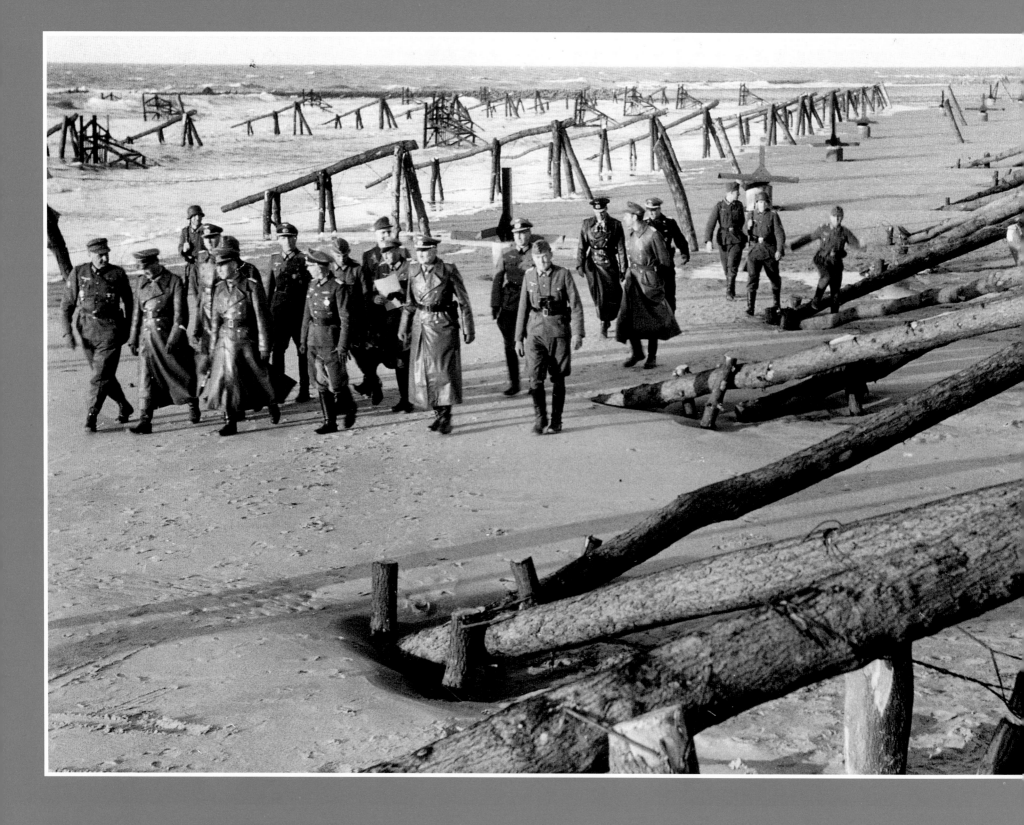

Rommel's imagination comes to the aid of the Atlantikwall

Marshal Rommel, surrounded by his staff and the officers in command of the units stationed in the sector, during an inspection of the Seine Bay beaches in February 1944. Following his visit, most of the obstacles were equipped with mines.

Ceaselessly travelling up and down the coast between the Escaut and the Loire estuaries, Rommel turned his attentions to the defensive buildings construction programme. During his first visits to the Atlantic Wall's construction sites he was taken aback by the overall inadequacy of the system. He was determined not to see his defeat at the hands of the British at El-Alamein repeated, and spared no effort in preparing for victory on the beaches, which both sides' strategists considered decisive for the conflict's final outcome. He particularly deplored the lack of adequate protection for the artillery, leaving as it did an unacceptable number of canons exposed, and multiplied inspection visits in attempts to accelerate construction, which he sometimes amplified, ordering supplementary forts or protection in different places.

But, as he could not use the armoured divisions as he wished, and as he only had a handful of high quality infantry divisions, he was very attentive to the beach defences and their immediate environment. He ordered obstacles of all shapes and sizes, some of which he invented himself, to be placed in both these zones. Within a few months, the coast underwent a veritable metamorphosis.

At the lowest limit of the tide, little, mined, wooden rafts were chained to stakes and floated just under the water's surface. On the beaches, the inter-tidal zone was strewn with some 500,000 obstacles, such as stakes, rails, tripods made of tree trunks, steel and concrete tetrahedrons, «Czech hedgehogs», «Belgian doors» two metres high; these were generally equipped with explosives, and designed to wreck any boat which might attempt to approach the beach. Higher up the beaches, artillery batteries were set in the sand, in positions where they could rake the shore.

In the dunes, kilometre upon kilometre of barbed wire and a multitude of anti-tank and anti-personnel mines were placed to hinder the progress of landed troops, and keep them under fire from the mortars, flame-throwers, and heavy machine guns equipping the bunkers built along the shore. The seawalls supporting the seaside towns' seafront promenades were extended with low concrete walls, resulting in solid anti-tank ramparts that would prove difficult to surmount.

Lastly, inland, the low-lying areas were flooded to hamper the landing of gliders and the dropping of paratroops. Elsewhere, flat open spaces without obstacles were covered in «Rommel's asparagus», 2 to 3-metre-high stakes. They were mined and joined up by wire, which triggered the explosives when an object hit them.

Palisades on the Morsalines beach (north-eastern coast of the Cotentin).

Spaces on the beaches and the open areas inland were blocked by «Rommel's Asparagus». Most of these were equipped with explosives, and were intended to prevent boats approaching the shore, and gliders landing in the fields.

«Rommel's Asparagus» carrying a Teller mine (detail).

«Czech Hedgehogs», so-called because of their origins: the Germans had retrieved them from the Czechoslovakian pre-war fortifications. They were invisible at high tide, and were intended to pierce landing barges' hulls; those on Omaha beach were to prove deadly.

Anti-personnel and anti-tank mines were everywhere along the shore. The Germans placed millions of them along the beaches, dunes, and in a band stretching six kilometres inland.

3. Monday 5th June: the last hours of a long eve of battle

In England, where General de Gaulle had arrived the previous day from Algiers on Churchill's invitation, the preparations were completed; the troops were ready. In Portsmouth, shortly after midnight, the commanders of SHAEF were assembled once more in the great library in Southwick House, Allied naval HQ; twenty four hours previously, a violent storm in the Channel had forced them to postpone the operation, and recall the boats which had already left port.

Shortly after 4 o'clock, after having gone round the table a last time, when the different opinions concerning the wisdom of going ahead and making the most of the lull announced for the next day had been aired, General Eisenhower decided: operation Neptune, the naval phase of Overlord, would once again be launched half way through the day; the assault on the Normandy beaches would begin at dawn the next day.

The disastrous meteorological conditions that plagued the Allied commanders were of course pleasing to their opposite numbers in the *Wehrmacht*. Taking note of the speed of the wind, and the state of the sea, the latter could consider the next few days with satisfaction: surely, they had no landings to worry about in the immediate future. As a result, and to allow the troops to relax and take a break from the many

The afternoon of the 5ᵗʰ of June. Boats of all sizes left the English ports, laden with men and equipment, on a moderately heavy sea.

The boats first headed for the arranged assembly point at sea – which was soon referred to as 'Picadilly Circus', due to the number of boats crowding there – then regrouped in convoys before heading for the Normandy coast, under battleship escort.

The crossing was to prove difficult for the men. Many were badly seasick, to the point of being severely physically diminished by the time they came within sight of the beaches, on which they were to do battle.

emergency exercises which had filled the previous few weeks, that of the night between the 5th and 6th June was cancelled. For their part, certain high-ranking officers were so sure of the improbability of an Allied operation that they did not hesitate in momentarily abandoning their command posts. By chance, Field-marshal Rommel, who had planned the journey several weeks previously, was one of their number, and set off for Germany at daybreak. His purpose in making the journey was double: he wanted to meet with Hitler, to ask him to bring the armoured divisions closer to the Seine Bay coasts; and he wanted to spend a day at home with his son and wife, whose birthday was on the 6th. Admiral Krancke, chief of the western naval group, was on a tour of inspection in Bordeaux; General Feuchtinger, commander of the 21st Panzer division, an armoured unit posted near Caen, was visiting his mistress in Paris. Finally, half a dozen generals, division commanders on the Normandy coast, had already left for Rennes, where they were to participate in an exercise involving map-based manoeuvres starting the next day, and which had long been planned by General Dollman, commander of the 7th Army.

At the end of the afternoon, while Field-marshal Rommel was with his family in Herrlingen, the Allied ships were leaving the English ports and converging on the rallying point at sea, south of the Isle of Wight, from whence they would reach the Normandy coast in convoys, under the protection of escorting battleships. Early that evening, General Eisenhower went to the Newbury-Exeter area to meet the «Screaming Eagles» of the 101st US Airborne. He had come to wish the American paratroops good luck, and spent the hours preceding their departure chatting with them.

Meanwhile, in London, and as it had for months, the BBC was broadcasting sibylline messages to the Resistance movements fighting the occupying Germans. The content of those diffused that evening around 9 o'clock – « Les carottes sont cuites » (The carrots are cooked), «Les dés sont sur le tapis» (The dice are cast), «Les sanglots longs des violons de l'automne bercent mon coeur d'une langueur monotone» (The soughing sobs of autumn's violins soothe my heart with monotonous languor) - was a signal to the French Resistance that the invasion operations were under way. Where were they going to take place? Not one of them really knew, but the people to whom these strange messages were addressed melted into the night to accomplish their missions; one to place explosive charges, another to sabotage public installations. In Cherbourg, a team cut the telephone line that linked the town to the rest of the country; in Caen, the railwaymen destroyed the water pumps to stop the Germans from using the locomotives; elsewhere, railway lines were dynamited.

At the same time, in the north of France, Colonel Helmuth Meyer, who had also heard the verses taken from Verlaine's poem, was persuaded, as he had been for several weeks, that they meant that an Allied invasion was imminent. This chief of the German 15th Army's counter-espionage hurried to inform General von Salmuth, the army's commander, who was playing bridge in his HQ near Tourcoing. Without much ado, the latter ordered a state of emergency, and had his superior, Field-marshal von Rundstedt, in his HQ in St-Germain-en-Laye, informed of the situation, who in turn warned the OKW, the Wehrmacht's high

Evening of the 5th of June. General Eisenhower came to encourage the paratroops of the 101st US Airborne, the «angels with dirty faces», as they called themselves.
Faces blackened so as to be even less visible when they got down to work that night, they were preparing to board the planes that would take them over the Normandy coast, behind the Utah sector.

Night of 5th to 6th June. The paratroops – here American – boarded complete with sufficient equipment to be operational and independent from the moment they landed, but this equipment weighed around 80 kg. Those who had the misfortune to land in flooded areas found it difficult to avoid drowning.

Night of 5ᵗʰ to 6ᵗʰ June. Four officers of the British 6th Airborne synchronising their watches, shortly before setting off to mark out the landing zone for their 5th Brigade, which was to be dropped near Ranville, north-east of Caen.

command in Berlin. All in all, much as usual since weeks before, the information climbed the hierarchical ladder… before coming back down in the form of an order.

All the north-west sectors of the *Atlantikwall,* informed by tele-printer, were put on the alert, although many high ranking officials in the German Army were more than sceptical as to the validity of the information. Most still thought that the main attack would come on the Pas-de-Calais coast, and considered the operation must be a pre-liminary diversion from the main manoeuvres. Thus, in Berlin, no-one wanted to risk waking Hitler up in the middle of the night to give him von Rundstedt's message, asking for two armoured divisions to be sent to the Seine Bay, just in case…

So, while the commanders of the OKW dithered in Germany, D-Day had already begun in England. As the armada of Allied ships headed for the Normandy beaches to disembark men and equipment, planes carrying paratroops or towing gliders full of infantrymen and their gear were taking off from British aerodromes.

Night of 5th to 6th June. Paratroops of the British 6th Airborne smiling for the camera shortly before taking off and flying over the Sword sector of the coast near Caen, between the Orne and the Dives. Not all of these men, every one a volunteer for the mission, had the good fortune to capture their designated objectives. Some drowned in the marshes along the Dives river; others were captured by the Germans.

6th June 1944: the assault on « fortress Europe »

2

Left: *Atlantikwall.* An anti-aircraft battery squad on guard, as they were every night, on the beaches of the Utah sector… Little did they guess that the next few hours were to be like none they had ever seen.

American paratroopers preparing to jump, behind the Utah sector beaches.

On the other side of the Channel, the troops' long wait was over at last. Shortly before midnight, the units were flown over the Normandy hinterland. Some of these units who were close to their objectives accomplished their mission without encountering particular difficulties. For others, the victims of bad drops, the affair rapidly proved delicate and murderous.

At dawn, after a turbulent Channel crossing due to the state of the sea, the boats carrying the first wave of assault troops reached the Seine Bay beaches. Whereas those of the British sector were taken with relatively few major difficulties, the American sector beaches proved more demanding, particularly Omaha, where the attackers lost a great many of their number. By nightfall, the landed troops had consolidated their positions on the shores in all sectors and had succeeded in advancing inland to greater or lesser extents.

1. During the night: the vanguard of airborne troops

The missions entrusted to the paratroops and infantry brought to Normandy from the very first hours of D-Day focussed around preventing the arrival of German reinforcements in the landing zone by capturing villages, bridges and various key points here and there. These units were then to hold their positions until the arrival of the troops who had landed on the beaches. The Americans and the British arrived over their respective jump zones at almost the same moment, the former at the centre of the Cotentin peninsula, and the latter to the north-east of Caen.

The mixed fortunes of the British

Near Caen, 6ᵗʰ of June. In position on the Benouville Bridge since the middle of the night, the British airborne units north-west of Caen were reinforced early in the afternoon by the arrival of Lord Lovat's commandos, who had landed a few hours earlier on Sword.
In the background are the gliders that landed Major Howard's men right at the bridge, re-baptised «Pegasus Bridge» in honour of the British 6ᵗʰ Airborne, whose emblem is a winged horse.

0h20, six Horsa gliders, drawn by as many tractor planes, flew over the right bank of the Orne, with the men of the British 6ᵗʰ Airborne on board. After uncoupling the gliders carrying 180 infantrymen, sixty-odd paratroopers dropped into the night. While one Horsa got lost over towards the east, near the Dives, two others landed near the Ranville bridge over the Orne. Not far from there, the other three landed close to the Bénouville bridge, which crosses the canal from Caen to Ouistreham; one of them landed within a mere 50 metres of the bridge.

As soon as they had landed, the infantry went in to action. They took full advantage of their totally unexpected assault, and of the inattention of the sentinels, who were distracted by the noise of the Allied aerial bombardments. Major Howard's men captured the designated bridges in a matter of minutes, meeting little resistance.

At the same moment, however, fortune was not smiling on the paratroops. They were to have marked out the terrain with beacons to guide the planes bringing reinforcements, but some had not landed where they were supposed to. So, when the planes arrived on site half an hour later, the pilots only had the beginnings of a signalling system to guide them and the 3ʳᵈ and 5ᵗʰ Brigades of the British 6ᵗʰ Airborne made their drop over the right bank of the Orne in confusion.

0h50, fog, the blinding beam of the enemy's powerful projectors sweeping the sky, the lack of sufficient markings on the ground: all these factors contributed to confusing certain pilots, who were busy trying to avoid the fire of German anti-aircraft batteries. Amongst those pilots who found it difficult to see where they were, some mistook the Dives, further east, for the Orne. Thus did many paratroops land far from the planned landing zones.

Some landed in places that Rommel had had flooded and many of them drowned, drawn down by the weight of their equipment. Those who escaped drowning and others, who had had the luck not to land in water, tried to return to their rallying point as quickly as possible, but many only arrived during the morning, and others who had been disabled never made it at all. These others fell victim to skirmishing with enemy garrisons or detachments on patrol, and were amongst the first killed or captured on D-Day. All told, and only after a determined struggle through adverse conditions, no more than half the men of the two units actually succeeded in reaching their rallying points.

2h30, a group of men from the 5ᵗʰ Brigade entered Ranville, which by dint of this event, became the first village liberated by the British; others, who had managed to assemble sufficient explosives, left to blow up five bridges over the Dives. At the same time, a detachment of the 3ʳᵈ Brigade advanced on Merville, on the orders of Major Ottway. Their mission was to neutralise the coastal battery garrison 2 km inland from the beach, which was equipped with cannons powerful enough to create problems for the troops who were to land on the Sword beaches.

At 4h30 Major Ottway's men were ready for action. They launched their attack on the enemy position with 150 men, instead of the 600 initially planned, and nothing heavier than a machine gun. They captured the position after a quarter hour of very fierce fighting, often hand to hand, losing half of their number. A heavy toll of victims, for a bitter victory: when the survivors penetrated the artillery's protective pillboxes, they discovered 75 mm Czech weapons, barely capable of reaching the beaches, instead of the powerful guns they had expected!

Thus, not long before daybreak, the western flank of the landing zone was in the grip of British hands. General Gale, chief of the British 6th Airborne, who had landed in a glider near Ranville at 3h30, had every reason to be satisfied: the men in his division had accomplished all the missions with which they had been entrusted. For him, and for all those who had survived the night, the battle to control positions had begun. But neither he nor his companions could have guessed that the struggle would last until mid-August, nor that it would be so taxing nor so ferocious.

The mixed fortunes of the Americans

Less than 100 km from the British, who were waiting for reinforcements still at sea, and keeping an eye out for the German riposte, the Americans were less successful in their mission. Parachuted behind the *Utah* sector, into a zone where hedgerows linked the many marshes and areas of land flooded by the Germans, things began badly and got worse.

At 1h30, 800 transport planes, preceded by a hundred or so fighter planes, flew over the paratroop and glider drop zones, which 360 scouts had begun to mark out as soon as they had arrived in the area, a little more than an hour before. They were carrying the 82nd and 101st US Airborne Divisions, commanded by Generals Ridgway and Taylor, a total of about 13,000 men. The first was dropped near Sainte-Mère-Eglise, to capture the village and the bridges crossing the Merderet; the second, not far from Sainte-Marie-du-Mont, their mission being to conquer the terrain as far as the coast, and thus protect the first wave of troops landing in the Utah sector as they advanced inland.

The pilots did their best to avoid the anti-aircraft fire from the German batteries, whilst battling to control their planes in violent winds and hampered by thick fog and the lack of markings on the ground. Many of them left the formation, dodging this way and that, and found themselves far from the drop zones. So the paratroops did not know what kind of ground lay beneath them as they jumped and the two divisions were more spread out than usual.

Nevertheless, some units were dropped at precisely the intended spot, some too precisely. This was the case of the men of the 82nd US Airborne, who were dropped just over Sainte-Mère-Église, while the population was busy putting out a fire which had started in a house near the church, with the German garrison overseeing the operations. Those who were not killed as they descended and who did not perish in the flames were captured the moment they hit the ground.

In short, there was total confusion and the situation was close to disastrous. The drops, which were hurried and imprecise, resulted in the dispersion of the assailants over an area with a 20-km radius, and disabled a large number of men. Many died under enemy fire before they even touched the ground; some drowned; others were quickly captured, betrayed by the click-clack of the «clickers» they used to recognise each other during the rallying phase, once on the ground.

Those who were capable of making the rallying points tried to reach them promptly, but very few succeeded. On the morning of the 6th of June, only one thousand of the 6,600 men of the 101st US Airborne had managed to join their units. Those incapable of doing likewise or who were too far away, had to improvise. Isolated, or in small groups, they wandered for days in search of their units, through fields and from village to village, all the while attempting to avoid the German patrols, resolutely and fervidly hunting them down. Contrary to the British, the American paratroops, which had come *en masse* to strike hard, gained very little from the element of surprise they had counted on.

Nevertheless, some units, often made up of men from both divisions, succeeded in taking the main points of passage and drove the enemy out of some key positions, through a combination of individual exploits and collective audacity. Some, and not the least important, were

North-east Cotentin, 6th of June. Not all the gliders had such lucky landings. Some, loaded with men, anti-tank guns, Jeeps and munitions, were smashed, unable to avoid the trees and hedges; others were overturned. This US Army Waco reached Hiesville at 5h45. It was one of a convoy of a hundred such gliders carrying infantrymen in support of the paratroops in position in the Utah sector.

gained in the face of little opposition. Thus, at 4h30, two hundred paratroopers of the 82nd US Airborne under the command of Colonel Krause entered Sainte-Mère-Eglise. Most of the men in the German garrison had fled the town, suddenly panicked at the idea of being surrounded. For the Allies, this village was the key to blocking the arrival of German reinforcements on the Utah beaches.

At dawn, many American units were in a precarious or, worse, a critical situation. Even if they were far from having achieved all their objectives, they had nevertheless captured the positions essential for things to run to plan during the day that was just beginning. Additionally, and by chance rather than good planning, their unintentional and extreme dispersion over the terrain, which had at first been a severe handicap, turned to their advantage. Their omni-presence, in small groups over a wide area, contributed considerably to wreak disorder and panic in the Germans' defence operation in the Cotentin.

2. At dawn: the massive assault on the beaches

The final bombardment of the Normandy coast took place in the last hours before daybreak. 1,130 British bombers dropped 5,800 tonnes of bombs between Cherbourg and Le Havre, then handed over to 1,080 American bombers which dropped a further 1,760 on the landing sites. Finally, around 5h30, the battleships, which had reached a position where the coastal guns were within range, went into action bombarding the German defences in their turn.

When dawn broke over the Seine Bay on the 6th of June, the occupying army's lookouts who had scanned the maritime horizon for months, were stricken by what they saw: a horizon choked by thousands of boats of all sizes and types. Battleships, transport ships and landing barges were before their eyes, a few hundred yards off shore. At that moment, a number of them were seized by a sentiment close to dread, as they witnessed the surreal spectacle of this huge armada inexorably drawing near.

On the German side, from sentinel to sector commander, all were completely taken by surprise. The garrisons posted on the coast were already stunned by the fiery deluge of steel that had rained down on them throughout the night, and their morale was badly rattled by the sight of such a swamping tidal wave of men and equipment. Faced with this spectacle, some of them felt little inclination to fight: these units composed of older German soldiers and the «Eastern volunteers», as they were at Utah and Gold, surrendered without much ado, bags packed and obviously ready to be taken captive. Contrariwise, through conviction or perhaps patriotism, others prepared to put up vigorous resistance and, undaunted by overwhelming odds, were resolutely decided to sell their lives dearly.

The Seine Bay, dawn on the 6th of June. The dense silhouette of the Allied fleet became visible in the German coastal guards' binoculars. Heavy and slow, it advanced inexorably...

Utah beach, 6h30. In this sector, from the Varaville dunes to those at Sainte-Marie-du-Mont, everything was so quiet that the GIs of the 8th Regiment of the 4th Infantry left the water with their rifles slung over their shoulders. They rapidly took control of the beaches, thanks to very weak German opposition.

During the morning. While some men snatched a few moments of respite in the shelter of the anti-tank wall running the length of the beach, others crossed it to get into the dunes.

Utah and Omaha, the American sector beaches

The troops were to land on the American sector beaches at 6h30, one hour after low tide. Shortly before 6h00, while the patrol boat which was to have led the assault boats in to the Utah beaches sank after colliding with a mined raft, the barges carrying the men were swept away by a strong cross-current, distancing them from the beaches where they were supposed to land. In spite of this, the first detachments of the American 4th Infantry set foot on the sand at the arranged time.

Far from being a problem, this unexpected development was beneficial. They had landed in a relatively weakly fortified coastal sector, being just next to the flooded areas inland. The only threatening object in sight was one pillbox containing a strangely silent gun. So the astonished troops disembarking from the first barges waded the hundred metres or so to the shore incredulously, to the sound of gently breaking waves, boats' engines and those of the handful of tanks they had with them.

In a brief space of time, some 600 men had rallied on the beach, among them General Theodore Roosevelt, the American president's eldest son and lieutenant commander of the 4th Infantry, and the only officer of his rank to land in the first wave of assault. He had insisted that it be so, declaring to his superiors that «*It'll reassure the boys to know I'm with them*». Before the men with him left the beach, he led them in an attack on the fortified position overlooking the beach. They made short work of the pillbox: a good number of them rushed the position following a well-adjusted tank shot, and took it without serious losses. Soon afterwards, they headed inland towards the paratroopers of the 101st Airborne, linking up with them around 13h00.

Fifteen kilometres further east, in the Omaha sector's sand dunes, the sea was rougher than elsewhere and the circumstances radically different. The American troops landing there were confronted by very different, difficult conditions. The Omaha sector was not only more heavily fortified than the Utah sector; it was also better defended. The units of the German 352nd Infantry posted there were superior soldiers to their counterparts of the 716th Infantry who they had replaced, or those of the 709th Infantry in position around Sainte-Mère-Église. Moreover, the men of the American 1st and 29th Infantry had to make the shore without cover from their tanks, which had for the most part sunk under the two metre-high waves the moment they left the ships.

During the afternoon. The American columns advanced without encountering any real difficulties. Only the marsh crossings and the areas voluntarily flooded by the Germans seemed able to slow their progress.

At 6h35, while the barges carrying the first units were still 400 metres from the beach, the German coastal defences, miraculously spared by the night's bombardment, started firing. Shells exploding in the water made the barges pitch even more, and machine gun fire lashed the boats' hulls. These men set off for the beach deafened by the noise of the infernal cannonade, and under a hail of bullets. Many of them never made it, easy targets moving with lumbering slowness through of the waves under the weight of their equipment. Those who did get to the shore were numb from the ordeal, and chilled to the bone. On the beach, there was extreme confusion. The rare tanks that had escaped collective shipwreck attacked the coastal batteries, which continued firing out to sea; some, which had been hit, caught fire and belched thick, black smoke. Even the many veterans of the landings on Sicily and Salerno who huddled under the German positions with their companions were limp with shock, and as if petrified by the awful scene assailing their eyes and ears. As the time went on, the landing turned to chaos: the barges and the troops crowded the beaches, jostling for position with floating bodies and wrecks brought in by the tide.

By 8 o'clock the situation was catastrophic. The troops, who were still coming in, were wiped out or pinned down by the enemy fire. However, the few surviving officers reorganised what was left of their units to impose decisiveness. General Norman Cota, lieutenant commander of the 29th Infantry Division, dragged them out of their torpor, urging his troops to move out in small groups and resolutely heading inland, Colt in hand, indifferent to the bullets whistling round him. Before following suite, Colonel Taylor, commander of the 16th Infantry Regiment, galvanised his men, declaring that there were «...two sorts of men who will stay on this beach: the dead and those who are going to die! Let's get out of here fast!» A few men fell in behind them, then a few more. Little by little, and sustaining heavy losses, the landed troops managed to get over the dunes. As the hours went by the German opposition dwindled, weakened by the support of two destroyers, which drew close to and destroyed the coastal batteries. Lacking reinforcements and fresh munitions, they were finally neutralised and the shadow of failure, which had seemed inevitable, lifted from Omaha at the end of the morning.

Omaha beach, 6h30. Between Vierville and Colleville-sur-Mer, where the fire from the German batteries was particularly heavy, the clash was much more violent. Buffeted by the heavy swell, the landing barges tried to steer a course between the obstacles blocking the approaches to the beaches.

Up to their armpits in water, the men in the assault brigades of the American 1ˢᵗ Infantry made heavy going towards the shore. Most were killed before they even got there, due to a lack of sufficient tanks. Only five amphibious tanks out of thirty-one succeeded in accompanying them, the others having sunk when they left the landing craft.

7 o'clock. A second wave of assault came within reach of the shore. The men in this second wave could see a narrow band of sand, covered with a thick cloud of smoke, and already strewn with corpses.

The infantrymen, weighed down under their kit, reached the beach under fire from automatic weapons, anti-tank guns and mortars. Some tried to advance more quickly by swimming and crawling straight ahead; others advanced sporadically, going from one obstacle to the next.

Sheltering from the fire from the coast behind the
«Czech Hedgehogs» they reached, the men who had
disembarked tried to get rapidly out of the water, so
as not to be caught by the rising tide. Not all of them
succeeded. For hours, the bodies of the dead served as
protection for the living, who were kept at some
distance from the beach for a long time. Until the
middle of the morning, all those who landed at
Omaha went through hell.

Among those who reached the beach, many got there exhausted or wounded. These men managed to reach the beach on an inflatable dinghy, after escaping from their shipwrecked landing craft.

During the last hours of the morning, the power and the determination of the German riposte caused heavy losses in the attacking forces: 2,500 killed or wounded, six times more than at Utah. Towards nine o'clock, the situation on the Omaha beaches was so catastrophic that General Bradley, commander of the American ground forces, out at sea on board the flagship USS Augusta, was very seriously worried. He was so anxious about the extreme confusion on the beaches and the turn of events that he sent an urgent message to General Eisenhower requesting permission to abandon the landing operation. But, by the time the message had reached Eisenhower in the afternoon, it was irrelevant, having been cancelled by another. While he waited for a reply, the troops, who had continued to land, had managed to leave the beaches and start moving inland.

A fortified position dominated the beaches between these two sectors. It had been built on the top of the cliff of the Point du Hoc, and supposedly housed six powerful guns within range of Utah and Omaha beaches, capable of foiling any attempted landing of troops. It was for this reason that 225 Rangers of the American 1st Infantry, under the command of Colonel James Rudder were given the task of making sure that the bombardments had destroyed it. To achieve this objective, they were to get there directly by scaling the cliffs.

At 7h10, 40 minutes later than planned, the Rangers were ready to start. Their barges' pilots, who also had to contend with strong crosscurrents, were obliged to bring their barges into a precise spot, unlike those at Utah. Colonel Rudder's men lost no time in covering the few metres separating them from the base of the cliffs, under the unwelcome fire of German machine guns thirty metres above them, while two destroyers offshore shelled the cliff-top intensely in the hope of keeping the 200 Germans stationed there at bay in their bunkers. But when the shelling stopped, to allow the Rangers to begin climbing, the defenders rushed out of their shelters and rained bullets and grenades down on them as they hauled themselves up the cliff-face.

Nevertheless, the assault did not last long. The first three Rangers reached the top in under five minutes and opened fire on the defenders positioned at the edge of the cliff, driving them back into their bunkers. Then, as their number grew, they forced the Germans to withdraw and took the battery, which had been deserted by most of its defenders and was… empty of guns.

The Pointe du Hoc. These sheer cliffs, 30 m high, were the theatre of operations of the 2nd Ranger US Infantry Battalion.

Pointe du Hoc, 6h00. Bombers of the 9th US Air Force bombing the German fortified positions.

Pointe du Hoc, 7h10. On the shingle beach, Colonel Rudder's men were preparing to scale the cliffs; rope ladders with grappling irons were fired onto the top of the cliffs by rocket from the landing craft 300 m offshore.
Ferocious and furious, the assault was reminiscent of a mediaeval siege launched against the ramparts of a stronghold.

Gold Beach, 7h52. With the support of the Funnies – here, a bridge carrier – the British 50th Infantry's assault brigades landed between Ver-sur-Mer and Asnelles. The main body of troops arrived shortly afterwards. The 25,000 men who landed made rapid progress inland all day long, but those who were heading for Bayeux were halted on the outskirts of the town just before nightfall.

Gold, Juno, Sword the Anglo-Canadian sector beaches

The British troops who landed in the Gold sector were given the mission of crossing the *Route Nationale* 13, taking Bayeux, then linking up with the Americans to the west and the Canadians to the east. The first to appear were the men of the 50th Infantry accompanied by a brigade of the 8th Armoured Division. Having covered themselves in glory at El-Alamein in 1942, then again in Sicily in 1943, they had come to exact retribution for the humiliation they had suffered four years previously, almost to the day, when they had been forced to flee Dunkirk.

In the boats, many men were badly affected by sea-sickness and were aware that they were not to have the advantage of preliminary action by their amphibious tanks, which had not been launched at sea, because of the sea state, but would be landing with them. However, the atmosphere on board was cheerful. Contrary to the Americans, who approached the shore pensively, the British joined in singing the choruses of the popular songs broadcast over the barges' loudspeaker systems. Choirs of hundreds sang songs such as «The gang's all here... We'll have a barrel of fun».

At 7h25, after their pilots had performed the feat of steering between the obstacles cluttering the already semi-submerged beach and under sustained fire from the coastal defences, the barges ran aground a hundred metres from the shore. West of Gold, the men of the 47th Royal Marine Commando quickly penetrated inland and were at Saint-Côme-de-Fresne, a hamlet half way to Omaha, by 8 o'clock. To begin with, at the centre of Gold, the assailants were stymied on the beach where the anti-tank battery in Le Hamel prevented the Allied tanks from making any progress. Mid-morning, one of them finally silenced the battery, by «posting a letter» – an

Above: **Juno Beach, 7h55.** Shortly after the first wave of men had opened breaches in the defences between Courseulles and Saint-Aubin-sur-Mer, with help from the «funnies», the units of the Canadian 3rd Infantry landed near Bernières.

Cables had been put in place to help the heavily loaded men, wading to the shore in water up to their chests and with bicycles over their shoulders. Their bicycles were supposed to permit them to reach Caen before nightfall, but proved of little use, due to the stout opposition of the German forces rallied round the capital of Lower Normandy.

Opposite: the men of the 48th Royal Marine Commando unit, who landed at Saint-Aubin to protect the flank of the beachhead beyond Bernières, were equipped with folding motorbikes, the Famous James, also used by the paratroops.

expression used by the 79th Armoured Division – in other words, firing directly into the bunker's slit so that the shell literally blew out the gun and the crew inside. At midday, thanks to the use of the «Crab» and «Petard» tanks, several passages had been opened towards the interior. The British began the massive movement on Bayeux, towards the Americans who had landed at Omaha.

Juno, in the centre of the Anglo-Canadian sector, was mainly attacked by Canadians, many of whom were motivated by the desire for revenge for the failed raid on Dieppe in August 1942. By the end of the day, they were to have established contact with the British, who had landed on either side of them, and captured the Carpiquet aerodrome, 8 km west of Caen. This ambitious mission did not begin under the best auspices. The sea was rough, as it was elsewhere, and the many reefs running along this part of the coast added to the difficulty of navigating around the obstacles put in place by the Germans. The barges' pilots were obliged to be doubly vigilant and sail at very low speed, but even so, and in spite of the precautions they took, nearly one third – 90 out of 306 – of the boats were destroyed before even reaching the shore.

At 7h55, nearly half an hour behind schedule, the Canadian 3rd Infantry landed before the tanks under heavy fire from the coastal defences, which had been left pretty much unscathed by the night's bombardments. In total, approach by sea and landing on the shore taken together, the 950 killed, wounded or missing made Juno the bloodiest beach in the Anglo-Canadian sector. But once they landed, General Hobart's funnies performed marvels from the moment they went into action. In under an hour, and with infantry support, they drove three passages through the minefields, barbed wire and block-houses to allow the first units ashore to leave the beach.

Courseulles was liberated at 9h30, then Bernières and Saint-Aubin at 10 o'clock and 11h30 respectively. However, the assailants had to resort to violent street fighting to wrest the latter two seaside towns from the grasp of the sector's defending German units, who put up a particularly fierce fight. In addition to blocking the arriving reinforcements on the beach, the enemy's resistance also slowed the Canadians' southward progress, towards Caen. Their hopes of reaching the Carpiquet aerodrome before nightfall dwindled as the day wore on.

Bernières. Leaving the beaches, Canadian infantry units headed for Bény-sur-Mer, with support from the amphibious tanks that had managed to reach the shore.

Saint-Aubin-sur-Mer. In streets blocked by the
retreating Germans, the men of the Canadian
8th Brigade advancing house by house, weeding
out snipers in ambush.

Sword, the easternmost sector of the landing zone, was the most threatening of all the beaches, as it was potentially the most heavily defended. The troops who landed there would be at the mercy of the *Kriegsmarine's* rapid offensive ships, Le Havre being only thirty kilometres away; on top of that, the 21st *Panzerdivision,* an armoured unit of battle-hardened men, many of whom had served under Rommel in North Africa, was in position not far from the coast, to the south-east of Caen. In order to limit the enemy's opportunities to counter attack with navy and armour, a good number of Royal Navy destroyers were on patrol off the coast and the British 6th Airborne had been parachuted deep inland before dawn.

At 7h25, the first troops of the British 3rd Infantry landed. With support from the Lord Lovat's 1st Special Brigade, they were to establish contact with General Gale's men, who had been in control of the bridges east of Caen since the middle of the night. They were then to take the town together, and thus gain access to the plain and the road that ran east towards the Seine and Paris. Again thanks to effective support from General Hobart's funnies, the commando attacks dealt quickly with the coastal defences. But the access routes inland were few and far between, and before long the beaches were jammed with men and tanks. The seeming confusion that set in progressively along the beaches was not dispelled until mid-morning, when the «Crab» tanks succeeded in opening four passages through the minefields. The infantry then took Hermanville, about 9h30, after fierce fighting during which 600 of their number were killed or wounded. Colville-sur-Orne fell in its turn, but without difficulty. Further east, in Ouistreham, where there were violent clashes, it was nearly mid-day before the Allies mastered their German adversaries.

Sword Beach, 8h45. After arriving on land however they could, the units of the British 3rd Infantry regrouped on the beach before heading for Hermanville. However, the stiff resistance put up by the coastal defence garrisons hampered their progress. It took the commandos three hours to take the «La Brèche» fortified dugout defending the sector.

Sword Beach, 8h45. Still stuck on the shore, troops sheltering from enemy fire behind tanks. In the foreground, a «Petard» tank.

Sword Beach, mid-morning. Equipped with propellers and flotation devices – here, in a lowered position – DD or Duplex Drive tanks were launched a few hundred yards from the coast. After reaching the shore under their own steam, they drove down the streets of Ouistreham as backup for the men of the 1st SSB who had taken the town.

It was here, in this seaside town, which the Germans had transformed into a veritable fortified camp, that the men of the Commander Philippe Kieffer's 1st Battalion of *fusiliers marins* (marines) distinguished themselves. They were the only French unit involved in the land-based operations on D-Day, and took the «casino» that morning, after an assault which left half of them dead or wounded. After this valiant feat of arms, those still able to continue fighting headed for Bénouville Bridge. Lord Lovat's men did likewise, while his piper played 'Blue Bonnets over the Border' to inspire courage in the troops, and cover the staccato rattle of machine gun fire. Towards 2 o'clock in the afternoon, both units met up with the British already in position on Bénouville's Pegasus Bridge.

Amfreville, mid-afternoon. Among the troops landed on Sword beach were the 177 Frenchmen of Lieutenant Philippe Kieffer's 1ˢᵗ Battalion of Marines. This unit of the Free French Forces, attached to Lord Lovat's 1ˢᵗ SSB, arrived on the Colleville-sur-Mer beach shortly before 8 o'clock. It was mainly made up of Bretons and Normans who had joined General de Gaulle in 1940, and distinguished itself taking the Ouistreham-Riva-Bella «Casino», a fortification built by the Germans on the site of the gaming establishment.

After having joined the men of the British 6ᵗʰ Airborne on Bénouville Bridge, the French Green Berets headed for Amfreville, where they were stationed several days, and repelled a German counter-offensive on the 10ᵗʰ.

WAR IN CHARCOAL

Manuel Bromberg participated in D-Day as the US Army's official artist, charcoal in one hand, and rifle in the other. This painter, illustrator and sculptor, born in 1917 in the US, landed on the Normandy coast on the 6th of June 1944, with the mission to bring back «a graphic illustration of the war». Sketched on the spot, his drawings are very little like those generally brought back from similar circumstances. These drawing represent neither combat nor visions of heroism, but rather an evocation of the suffering endured on the battlefield. Voluntarily imprecise, the lines of the drawings suggest men, places and situations with a confirmed eye for movement.

3. Throughout the day: combat on land and the bombardment of towns

Once the positions on the beaches had been consolidated, some taking longer than others, the landed troops applied themselves to establishing contact with those who had landed near them, or who had been flown in during the night. The Allied units which had got a foothold in Normandy now turned their efforts to the establishment of bridgeheads to further the continuous arrival of reinforcements and equipment.

On the German side, the counter-attack was a long time coming, but once their surprise had been digested and the shilly-shallying of the top brass was at an end, the reaction of the reserve troops ordered to counter the assailants, for all it was belated, was particularly pugnacious.

At dawn, the German coastal defence garrisons had not succeeded in repelling the first waves of assault, nor hindering their progress inland during the morning.

On the German side: the chiefs' procrastination and measured recourse to reinforcements

At 9h15, as the first international communiqué broadcast by the SHAEF confirmed to the whole world that: «under the command of General Eisenhower, and with considerable air support, the Allied navies began landing the Allied armies on the northern coast of France this morning», and that the Allied troops were continuing to pour onto the Normandy beaches, consternation and exasperation were at their height in the German coastal sector command posts. With their knowledge of the terrain, all the German commanders quickly realised that this was a momentous situation. Consequently, those who still could telephoned Marshal von Rundstedt's HQ incessantly, urging him to send reinforcements, particularly tanks. But, while refusing to call Hitler personally (he despised Hitler), he did not dare give the reserve divisions the order to attack, as he was convinced that he would not be obeyed if, by chance, his orders should overstep the Führer's instructions.

In the Cotentin, at the beginning of the afternoon, the Germans, who had fallen back and were awaiting reinforcements, were organising their defensive lines.

In Germany, a little after 10 o'clock, Hitler, who had just risen, learned the news without showing any surprise. After having read the first reports drafted by the German intelligence service and consulted maps, he declared to the several Nazi dignitaries around him that it was a mere diversion, a practice run for the real Allied invasion, which most of them expected to come further up the coast, as they had for some time. In Herrlingen, Rommel was on the point of leaving home. He had been forewarned of the situation three hours previously by his chief of staff and had abandoned the idea of meeting the Führer, preferring to return directly to his HQ in La Roche-Guyon, near Pontoise.

At that moment in Normandy, the commander of the 21st *Panzer* received his first operational orders. General Feuchtinger who had personally put his troops on the alert immediately after he had been informed of the first British parachute drops, and had subsequently taken the initiative of a counter-offensive to the east of the Orne as early as 6h30, learnt that he «had to cease all movement of tanks against the paratroops and come west in support of the troops defending Caen.»

Towards 3 o'clock in the afternoon Hitler, perhaps less convinced than he had pretended to those around him, ordered two armoured divisions, the 12th *SS Panzer* and the *Panzer Lehr* respectively stationed around Argentan and Vimoutiers, to advance and take up positions near the Normandy coast. Simultaneously, 40 tanks of the 21st *Panzer,* which had reached the north of Caen, were getting ready to launch their second counter-offensive of the day. They headed in the direction of the sea, accompanied by infantry battalions, down the 8 km-wide corridor, which still separated the troops en route from Juno and Sword.

General Feuchtinger's tanks' progress was hindered half way. Most had to withdraw into the Lebisey woods, less than 5 km north of Caen, after having clashed violently with the first Allied tanks they had met. Their progress was delayed, but not checked, as a company of motorised grenadiers and six tanks, veering westward, reached the area around the Luc-sur-Mer beaches, at about 19h00. The chief of the 21st *Panzer* wished to make the most of this breakthrough, and dispatched reinforcements there. He brought in units from the 716th Infantry, stationed north-west of Caen, and added an extra fifty tanks or so to give the counter-attack substance. It was re-launched at sunset, but was short-lived.

It was the arrival of several hundred Allied planes in the Normandy sky, carrying troops and towing gliders, escorted by fighters, which made General Feuchtinger suddenly change his mind. He revised his appraisal of the situation, worried that their flight over the coast north-east of Caen had gone unchallenged by the coastal defences, and renounced pursuing the manoeuvre. The units that had advanced on Luc-sur-Mer were isolated, harassed, and could not count on the arrival of any support, so they too withdrew to avoid becoming surrounded. They made the Lebisey woods, where German tank crews and infantry had formed a solid defensive line, which had succeeded in thwarting the British attempts to enter Caen for several hours. How many British soldiers could have imagined that it was to take them no less than 33 days to overcome this obstacle?

East of the Orne estuary. The tanks of the 21st Panzer, which had counter-attacked the troops of the 6th Airborne as soon as dawn had broken, headed for the coast to halt the advance of the troops landed at Sword.

The towns targeted by Allied bombardments

As they were unable to capture Caen on the day of the invasion, the Allies accelerated the process of isolating Lower Normandy, in order to complicate the arrival of German reinforcements. So as night was falling, the region's principal towns were systematically bombed. Between 20h00 and 20h30 some 740 American bombers dropped 1,540 tonnes of bombs on their designated targets, but reconnaissance flights confirmed that these bombardments were none too accurate, the planes having flown at high altitude to remain out of range of the German anti-aircraft batteries, in spite of the low cloud ceiling. Judging that a second wave was necessary, Allied command sent in one thousand British bombers with an extra 3,500 tonnes of bombs between midnight and two in the morning. Ruined and burning, the towns had suddenly become the most coveted prizes for the armies of both camps. The population's long ordeal had begun.

In the space of two bombardments, in the Cotentin, Saint-Lô was virtually wiped off the map, and counted 400 dead; Coutances, two-thirds destroyed, mourned 350. In the Calvados department Lisieux, Condé-sur-Noireau and Vire, all ravaged by a deluge of bombs, lost 1,000, 250 and 400 respectively.

In Caen, the bombers had started doing their rounds at sunrise. At the moment when the first troops were landing on the beaches, the barracks and the station had already been hit. During the morning, the echo of distant fighting had fuelled the turmoil that had the town in its grip. Watched by the population torn between worry and hope, the German garrison had been deployed in the streets. Taking up position at crossroads, detachments had prepared machine gun and anti-tank gun batteries. At the same time, inside the prison walls, over eighty men and women resistance fighters arrested during the preceding weeks were summarily executed.

But it was at 13h30 that the Norman capital underwent one of its most punishing bombardments. A brief yet extremely violent raid resulted in the destruction of the areas around the bridges and the town centre; the *Monoprix* was hit and then consumed by fire. Columns of thick, black smoke were rising from the ruins and emergency teams and the passive defence agents were hurrying to and fro, when the bombers flew over the town again, at about 16h30.

When that terrible day drew to a close, 2,000 Caennais were dead, crushed under the rubble, burned alive or because rescuers hadn't been able to haul them clear in time, rescuers whose number quickly proved insufficient given the scale of the carnage. 10,000 others had left to take refuge outside the town. How many of them could have imagined that they would not be back for a month, and that the worst was yet to come?

Whereas General de Gaulle, on the BBC airwaves, was affirming that the Normandy landings signalled that the «supreme battle was joined», the martyrdom of Norman towns began.
Of course, some were liberated without suffering major damage, but many were seriously mutilated by the Allies' massive and repeated bombardments. Like Saint-Lô, Falaise and Caen, many were virtually totally destroyed. At the end of the day, only Bayeux was spared, doubtless thanks to the massive concentration of Anglo-Canadian troops stationed around the town on the evening of the 6th of June.

Above: St-Lô. *Below:* Falaise.

Caen, afternoon of the 6ᵗʰ of June. After the day's second wave of bombarment, the town was in flames. Here, the centre seen from the Abbaye-aux-Dames; on the left, the harbour and Place Courtonne; the Saint-Jean area is in the background.

Half way through the day's bombardments, a bomb hit the Monoprix supermarket. The firemen got there quickly and immediately attacked the blaze.

After the bombardments of the 6th of June, certain areas of Caen were prey to flames for days. Pro-Vichy and collaborationist German propaganda exploited the situation, and took advantage of it to vilify the Allies; the authorised newspapers, which echoed them, imitated them outspokenly and without hesitation.
This photo, taken at the junction of the Rue Saint-Jean and the Rue de Bernières, appeared in the press, with the caption: «The town of Caen, under Anglo-American bombardments, is in flames».

Caen, 6th June, end of the afternoon. While German soldiers cleared the rubble lying in the streets and preventing troop movements, the people of Caen, who were still shell-shocked, left the town to take refuge in the outlying countryside, with only meagre bundles for luggage.

In the Allied camp: an equivocal outcome, but a successful invasion

At nightfall, as Field-marshal Rommel reached his HQ in La Roche-Guyon, and German reinforcements converged on the coasts of Lower Normandy from all directions to stem the invaders' advance, the Allies had successfully established themselves. Apart from the 20,000 vehicles of all types, some 156,000 men, of whom 72,000 were American, had been transported by sea and air. Overall, the objectives in this domain had been achieved: the absence of a naval response and the quasi non-appearance of the Luftwaffe in the sector had allowed the Allies to achieve 90% of plan Neptune, although this was not the case of the whole Overlord plan proper, notably in the American Omaha sector.

At Utah, where the infantry and paratroopers of the US Army had succeeded in linking up, the results obtained were close to their objectives: the bridgehead was well organised and only a few pockets of German resistance remained.

At Omaha, the situation was still undecided. It was unlikely that they would be able to hold the beach, all the more so as the troops had hardly made any progress inland after landing. The coastal defence garrisons were dug in along a line about one kilometre from the beaches, and the fate of the Americans hung in the balance, to be decided by the speed of the German reinforcements' arrival. Nevertheless, the liberation of Saint-Laurent-sur-Mer around 18h00 meant that a start to work on the building of the artificial port planned there was still feasible the following day.

On the Pointe du Hoc, the rangers' situation was just as precarious. After having discovered the gun battery that the Germans had positioned a short way back from the cliffs shortly before, Colonel Rudder's men vainly awaited the arrival of reinforcements expected from Omaha, and repelled the fierce German counter-attacks alone. Isolated and left to fend for themselves, they made ready to spend the night in position around the battery they had conquered after their hard-fought struggle that same morning.

In the Anglo-Canadian sector, although they had achieved significant successes, not all of their objectives had been attained either. The British who had landed at Gold had succeeded in meeting up with the Canadians at Juno, but had failed to do the same with the Americans at Omaha. They were still 2 km from Bayeux, and the town was still in German hands, but the liberation of Arromanches meant that work on the building of the artificial port planned there could start the following day, on schedule.

At Juno, the Canadians had taken the front line well into the interior. Although they had made contact with the British at Gold, the same was not true on the Sword side; nor had they managed to capture the Carpiquet aerodrome, even though some men had made it as far as the runways.

At Sword, after having established a solid bridgehead around Lion-sur-Mer, the British had joined up with General Gale's men, who had taken up position inland during the night, but their progress was brought up short at the gates of Caen, D-Day's main objective.

Omaha, beginning of the afternoon. The confusion had lessened, but the fighting was still raging on the beaches, where half-tracks were towing anti-tank guns, soon to be used to force a passage. Inland, the troops that had landed in the morning were still finding deployment extremely difficult.
The beaches, which were now no more than narrow strips of sand, were littered with debris and wrecks of all descriptions.

Pointe du Hoc. Assailants under siege; Colonel Rudder's men waiting for reinforcements. They were to wait another whole day.

Sainte-Mère-Eglise. The star spangled banner had been flying over the town hall since 4h30, but there was still skirmishing. For the following 48 hours, Colonel Krause's men were to have to repel the counter-offensives of the Germans who had fallen back to the outskirts of the village just before their arrival, and neutralise the fire of those hiding in ambush inside the village.

Thus, as far as conquered territory was concerned, the results obtained by the Allies were not as extensive as had been hoped for, but the unequal progress of the landed troops could not conceal the main facts: the German coastal defences had been neutralised in many places, and nowhere had the assailants been forced back into the sea. In other words, the *Atlantikwall* had not foiled operation Overlord; the landings were a success. From that moment on, for the survivors of «the longest day», the Battle of Normandy had begun.

Right bank of the Orne, shortly after 8 pm.
Some 250 Horsa gliders landed around Ranville. On board men, jeeps, and anti-tank guns: support for the troops who had vainly been trying to take Caen since that morning.

The men of the 5th Engineers Special Brigade arriving at Omaha at the end of the afternoon, with orders to clean up the beach and build storage areas for equipment. They also helped with the evacuation of the wounded.

While the reinforcements continued arriving on the by now totally mine-free beaches of the American and Anglo-Canadian sectors, another flowing rotation of ships became established.

Approaching the shore with the rhythm of the tides, these boats were part of the provisioning system for the landed troops; some left with German prisoners on board.

La Cassine – fortified position (Juno Beach), end of the morning. While the Canadian wounded were being evacuated from the beach, the erstwhile defenders of the pillbox, now its prisoners, and showing the strain of the last few hours, were kept under surveillance, waiting to discover what was to become of them.

Sainte-Marie-du-Mont (Utah Beach), end of the morning. Grouped together inside a makeshift barbed wire enclosure on the beach, these German soldiers, caught during the morning, do not seem unhappy with their lot. Having escaped alive from the deluge of fire and steel, their war was not over, but the worst was behind them.

PRISONERS OF WAR: SOLDIERS WITH NEITHER WEAPONS NOR LUGGAGE

East of the Orne estuary, mid-afternoon. Paratroopers and airborne infantrymen of the 6th Airborne, who had been captured inland during the course of the morning, arriving in Saint-Pierre-sur-Dives, prisoners of the grenadiers of the 21st Panzer. After crossing the square in front of the abbey church, they were taken into the schoolyard. Much like their German counterparts, they wondered how long their captivity would last, and where they would be taken.
Over the next few days, German propaganda and the Vichy government made extensive use of these photos to attempt to persuade public opinion that the landings in the Seine Bay were a fiasco, just as the expedition to Dieppe had been, in 1942.

107

From the beaches to the «Falaise pocket»: the Battle of Normandy

3

The Allied superiority in the air played a cardinal role in the success of Operation Overlord and in that of the Battle of Normandy. The Allied bombardments cost the enemy dear, but reduced a great number of towns and villages in Lower Normandy to ashes.
Carpet bombing, a technique that was systematically applied before each offensive launched from July onwards, destroyed everything, be it men, equipment, or constructions, in a given sector, including soldiers in the liberating armies, due to the lack of precision with which some loads were dropped.

In spite of mixed results, the landing was a success for the Allies, but there was still much to be done before they could cross the Seine and enter Paris and, further on, Germany.

So, from the 7th of June, Normandy became the prize and the arena for a race between warring parties. The Allies piled in men and equipment of all sorts, in their bid to wrest it from the Germans, who fought to retain control by sending ever more reinforcements there, once they had accepted that this was the real invasion.

From June until August the massive and continuous influx of forces from both camps transformed Normandy into a vast battleground, where operation followed operation for twelve whole weeks. The assault on the beaches was succeeded by «hedgerow warfare» and the fight for control of the towns.

1. The defence of attained positions and extension of the bridgehead, 7th-27th June

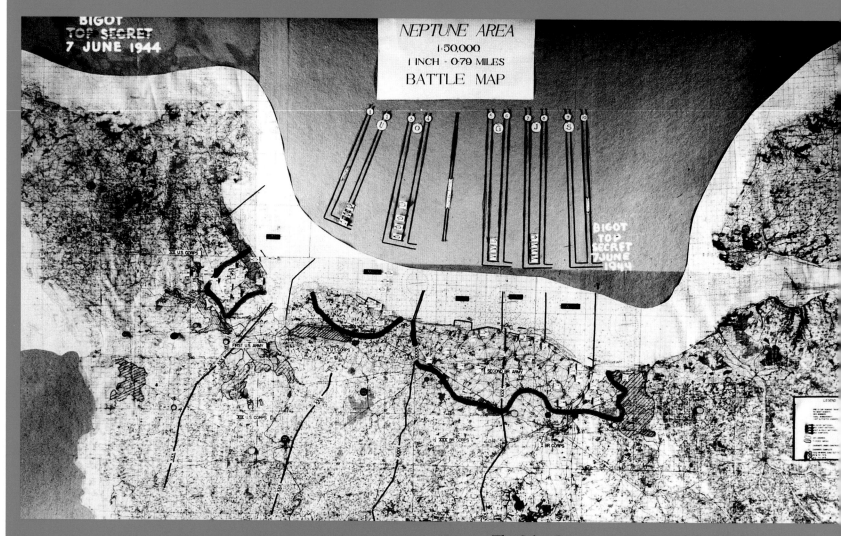

The Seine Bay coast, morning of the 7th of June.
The troops who had landed the day before had more or less succeeded in penetrating inland. However, and contrary to the objectives, links between the five sectors had not been consolidated and Caen was still firmly held by the German garrison there.

On the day after D-Day, Generals Montgomery, Bradley and Dempsey met on board a ship in position off the Normandy coast. Just before disembarking for the 21st Army Corps' tactical headquarters, they conferred on the prioritisation of the missions to be accomplished over the following few days, given the results obtained the previous day. The three men decided to complete the link-up between the different landing sectors and consolidate, then extend the bridgehead by multiplying offensives to maintain momentum and to keep the operational initiative; but the Allied troops' progress was to be slower, more difficult and bloodier than they imagined.

The consolidation exercise of the first days on land

As of the morning of the 7th of June, while the construction of the artificial ports had already begun off the Gold and Omaha beaches, the Anglo-Canadians multiplied their attacks around Caen, in order to take the town more rapidly, but the men of the British 3rd Infantry could not force a passage through the Lebisey sector, nor could the Canadians of the 3rd Infantry capture the indispensable Carpiquet aerodrome; the 12th *Panzer Hitlerjugend,* which had arrived during the night, rained bullets and shells down on them and made it impossible for them to move. Nevertheless, behind the lines, the British and the Canadians completed the task of closing the corridor which still separated the Juno and Sword sectors, the space into which had slid the front runners of the 21st *Panzer* the previous evening.

Further west, the British 50th Infantry, in position near Bayeux since the end of the day before, entered the town shortly after 8 o'clock. The former mediaeval capital was the first French town to be liberated, with little destruction and without much real fighting. A brief skirmish with the small German garrison, still in position in front of the Post Office, was sufficient to allow a column of British infantry to take control. Continuing to advance, the British crossed the *Route Nationale* 13 between Bayeux and Caen and headed for Villers-Bocage, with the intention of attempting to enter Caen. However, they were stopped in their tracks mid-way by heavy fire from the armour of the *Division Lehr* which, having come from Chartres, stood in their way at Tilly-sur-Seulles.

Wishing to see his troops, who were stuck, reach the gates of Caen rapidly, Montgomery dreamt up an operation to outflank them on the west, entrusting the task of trail-blazing to the tanks of the 7th Armoured Division, who had already distinguished themselves under his command in 1942 at El-Alamein. Unfortunately, on the morning of the 13th of June, the operation came to a sudden end. After having entered Villers-Bocage without encountering any resistance, the armour of the 22nd Brigade, the «Desert foxes», set off boldly along the road to Caen, where they were stopped after a short distance by a handful of tanks from the *Division Lehr,* which were keeping watch on the sector from a camouflaged position. The confrontation was short-lived, extremely violent and turned into a massacre. Under orders from Lieutenant *Waffen-SS* Michael Wittman, who had acquired the reputation of German tank-ace on the eastern front, five *Tiger* tanks, 55-tonne monsters, wiped out thirty British tanks, as many

Manche, 7th June. The Phoenix caissons, each of which was equipped with an anti-aircraft battery on its platform, after leaving the docks in England to cross the channel under escort. Towed at three knots, they were to be used to build the artificial ports off Saint-Laurent-sur-Mer and Arromanches.

Bayeux, 7ᵗʰ June. Main town of one of the administrative sub-divisions of the Calvados department, and situated 15 km from the beaches, the town was liberated, without being destroyed, by the men of the British 50ᵗʰ Infantry, who met practically no resistance. On the 12ᵗʰ of June, Eisenhower visitied it, followed on the 14ᵗʰ by General de Gaulle.

Southern outskirts of Bayeux, 7ᵗʰ June. Having crossed the RN 13, a column of tanks of the British 11ᵗʰ Armour headed with all speed to Tilly-sur-Seulles. On route, they came across a Spitfire of the Canadian 412ᵗʰ Squadron, which had been shot down.

North of Caen, dawn on the 7th of June. While the city burned, the 12th Panzer SS «Hitlerjugend» took up position in the sector between l'Abbaye-d'Ardenne and Lébisey, whence it was to counter-attack jointly with General Feuchtinger's 21st Panzer «to push the enemy who has landed back into the sea».
This armoured division of the Waffen SS, created in June 1943, was characterised by the extreme youth of its recruits, whose average age was 17. It joined the battle on the 7th of June and blocked the Canadians' progress towards Carpiquet until the 9th of July.

Pointe du Hoc, 8th June. After 48 hours spent in a most
perilous situation, Colonel Rudder's men were joined
by the units of the 29th Infantry. Their heroic but useless
assault, which has become part of the legend, was one
of the great feats of arms of the Normandy landings,
costing the lives of 135 of the 225 Rangers involved
in the operation.

armoured cars and 250 men, constraining what was left of the celebrated 7th Armoured Division to beat a chastened retreat.

At the end of the day, the exercise was a clear and bitter failure, but the consequences of this abortive attempt went far beyond its disastrous outcome. In its wake, the first hints of discouragement rippled through the troops and gave rise to doubts concerning the reasoning behind the tactics employed by high command. All the more so as General Bayerlein's armour, which arrived too late to stop the British seizing Bayeux, was to succeed in blocking all Allied progress at that point for over a month.

The situation was more confused in the Utah and Omaha sectors, where the landed troops now had to fight everywhere to conserve the terrain that had been won. The two camps' fighters, who were not facing each other over a line, were each engaged for a week in trying to enlarge the territorial enclaves that they controlled. For the Americans, this meant reducing the isolated pockets of German resistance, and linking their two landing zones, and joining up with those of the British who had come in to Gold.

To the east of the American sector, this objective was attained on the 8th of June. Towards midday, the units that had landed at Omaha reached the Pointe du Hoc, where they met Colonel Rudder's Rangers; that evening they reached Port-en-Bessin, which had been liberated that morning by the British Royal Marines. To the west, after 72 hours spent weeding out snipers in ambush and repelling the German counter-attacks on Sainte-Mère-Église, the paratroops of the 82nd US Airborne had a firm hold on the locality, strategically well situated to protect the routes off the Utah sector beaches and the road to Cherbourg. The Allies now needed to capture Carentan, the other key point situated further down the RN13.

The paratroopers of the 101st US Airborne and units of the American 2nd Armoured Division finally took Carentan, which had been evacuated by the German garrison, on the morning of the 12th of June after several days of fierce fighting. Colonel von der Heydte's 6th Parachute Regiment had been decimated by the fighting all around Carentan since the 6th of June and had abandoned the town the previous evening, as they were also very short of ammunition. They returned, however, the next day, in a violent counter-attack launched with support from reinforcements of the 17th *SS Panzer* grenadiers, but in vain. They were firmly repelled, and finally left; the American line was definitively consolidated. This success made the linking of the Utah and Omaha sectors possible, albeit once more at the cost of heavy losses.

Carentan, 12th June, 7 o'clock. Americans entering the town, which had been evacuated by most of the population three days beforehand.

Carentan, 13th June. Americans patrolling in the rubble of the station, which was destroyed on the 6th of June, after having repelled the German counter-attack. Carentan was considered a priority objective by the Allies, and was heavily bombarded several times, during which a hundred or so of its inhabitants were killed, including Dr. Caillard, the town's Mayor.

Carentan, 14th June. The linking of the Utah and
Omaha sectors had been achieved, but the Americans
were not to progress southwards for several weeks.
The wreckage of German and American military
vehicles on the road out of the town, interspersed
with the bodies of animals, blocking the road to Périers,
bore witness to the violence of the fighting there.

GENERAL DE GAULLE IN NORMANDY

14th June, morning. General de Gaulle left Portsmouth on board the destroyer La Combattante, with a handful of prominent figures from the Free French. He set foot on the shores of Normandy early in the afternoon, between Courseulles and Graye-sur-Mer, and so felt French soil for the first time in four years, nearly to the day, 48 hours after Churchill. After having met with Montgomery in his HQ in Creully, the leader of Free France went to meet the French, wondering what their reactions would be. Would they recognise him as their undisputed leader, he whose voice they had heard for the last four years?

15h30. General de Gaulle on his arrival in Bayeux. On reaching the premises of the local administration, he proceeded with the installation of the first Commissioner of the Republic, and charged the commissioner to administer the territories liberated from the Germans, in his name. After this, he went to the Place du Château, where he gave his first address in metropolitan France. He visited Isigny-sur-Mer, in the American sector, which had been almost totally destroyed and where he addressed comforting words to the population before leaving for England at the end of the day, following a visit to Grandcamp-les-Bains. Everywhere he went, de Gaulle was acclaimed, and congratulated. The General shook outstretched, congratulatory, grateful hands as he walked in the middle of a deeply moved and enthusiastic crowd.

This day of jubilation, this lightning visit to the Bessin, was General de Gaulle's opportunity to show Roosevelt, the US President, that the French people recognised his legitimacy - Roosevelt had not been persuaded by his claims to the head of the provisional French government. His triumphal reception by the Normans, a veritable popular plebiscite, was a precursor of that which he was to receive from the Parisians on the 26th of August in a liberated Paris.

«We are all moved to be here together in one of the first French towns to be liberated, but this is not the time to talk of emotions. The country expects you, behind the front, to continue to fight today, as you have never ceased to fight since the beginning of this war and since 1940. Our cry now, as it has always been, is a cry of combat, because the path of combat is also the road to liberty and to honour.

«This is the voice of the mother country. We shall continue to fight this war with our terrestrial, naval and airborne forces, as we are today fighting in Italy, where our soldiers have covered themselves with glory, as they shall tomorrow in France. Our empire, which is complete and gathered around us, is helping tremendously. We will fight for France with passion, but also rationally.

«You who have been under the boot of the enemy and have been part of the Resistance, you know what this war is about. It is a particularly hard war, this clandestine war, this war without weapons. I promise you that we will continue this war until the sovereignty of every square inch of French territory is re-established. No one shall prevent us from achieving that.

«We are fighting beside the Allies, with the Allies, as an ally. And the victory which we will win, will be the victory of liberty and the victory of France.

«Please join me in singing the national anthem, the Marseillaise.»

General de Gaulle, Bayeux, 14th June 1944

Bayeux, 14th June, Place du Château. Speaking into a microphone working off a van's battery, General de Gaulle addressing the many inhabitants of Bayeux who came to hear him. In front of the platform, Admiral d'Argenlieu and General Koenig, partly obscuring Maurice Schumann.

Isigny-sur-Mer, 14th June. Standing on a cart, General
de Gaulle preparing to speak to the population, who ran to see
the man whose voice had become so familiar over the years.

The uneven expansion of the bridgehead

Near Caen, the British 2ⁿᵈ Army was making ready to launch a new offensive to liberate the town and erase the memory of their failure at Villers-Bocage, which had given rise to the voicing of much criticism concerning the strategic choices made by Montgomery, who was still opposed to the idea of a frontal attack. General Dempsey thus planned to take Caen, in a westward movement, with considerable air support. This operation, baptised Epsom, was postponed on the very day it was supposed to start because of a violent storm which blew up on the 19ᵗʰ of June, making it impossible both for planes to take off, and to land reinforcements and equipment on the beaches.

At this time, the commanders of the German units in Normandy were disconcerted by the fact that the Allies did not simply advance straight forward after having broken through the defensive line on the beaches. Their anxiety grew as the days passed, as they realised that their repeated orders not to yield an inch of terrain had no hope of being followed. Moreover, Hitler, who still seemed to be under the influence of Fortitude, had made strategic choices that bore the hallmark of disregard for reality, not reassuring for the outcome of the battle. The requests for reinforcements that they addressed to the chiefs charged with the defence of the western front became more and more insistent.

Rommel and von Rundstedt, who had hitherto been opposed with regard to the manner of dealing with an Allied invasion, shared ever more similar points of view. They forgot the *Panzerkontroverse,* by now irrelevant, and both agreed that, as the battle of the beaches was already lost after a week of fighting, it was essential to send reinforcements to Normandy to delay the Allied victory there, in order to gain time to organise a strategic withdrawal to protect the Reich's territory. On the 17ᵗʰ of June, both men travelled to Margival, near Soissons, to meet the Führer in the hope of persuading him to change his tactics.

The interview took place in Hitler's concrete HQ, which he had had built as early as autumn 1940, to serve as an advanced command post in anticipation of the invasion to come from the British Isles. In spite of arguments forged on the anvil of the terrain's realities, the two field-marshals failed to convince Hitler of the validity of their analysis. Hitler was deaf to all opinions different from his own, and flung the responsibility for German setbacks on those who executed his orders. He had no intention of departing from the sacrosanct principle of never retreating that he had imposed since the start of the war, as long as he could persuade himself that the *Vergeltungswaffe,* the V1 rockets, which had been falling on London since the previous day, would beat Britain into submission and force the Allies to reconsider their plans with regard to Germany.

While the British and the Canadians struggled to wrest Caen from German hands, the Americans were discovering the terrors of «Hedgerow warfare» in the Cotentin. With support from their air force, the men of the American 1ˢᵗ Army relentlessly pushed the enemy backwards and the infantry of the 9ᵗʰ Infantry Division captured Barneville on the 18ᵗʰ of June. Having reached the west coast, the Americans achieved more than merely liberating a few more towns and villages. By isolating the northern third of the peninsula, they succeeded in trapping the 40,000 Germans there, at the same time increasing their chances of rapidly capturing Cherbourg which, as the days passed, became an ever more pressing objective.

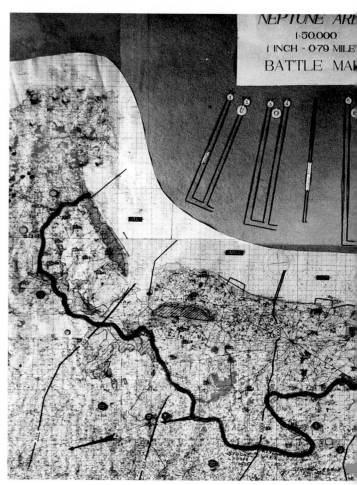

D-Day + 7. The Allies, who now controlled the zone between the right bank of the Sinope, near Quineville, and the left bank of the Dives, had an unbroken bridgehead in the Seine Bay. It was around 100 km long, and stretched inland over a distance of between 10 and 30 km.

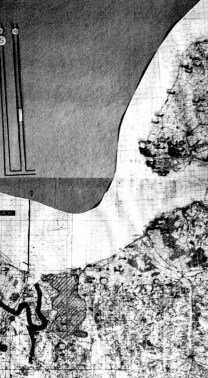

Saint-Lô, 14th June. Captured during the first week of the battle, paratroopers of the 101st US Airborne, sure of their army's strength, placidly waiting to be delivered. The Germans treated their prisoners well, as they shared the same convictions, and knew that their roles were soon to be exchanged.

Tanks and other armoured vehicles covered with
branches, blending into the hedgerows, like
chameleons. Their teams' only real fear was of the
Allies' air raids.

Whereas the American and British air forces were everywhere during the battle, the Luftwaffe was conspicuous by its absence both on D-Day and afterwards. The German ground forces, who knew that they had no real air cover, dreaded the appearance of the Allied fighter-bombers, which invariably resulted in heavy losses for them. The Jabos – abbreviation for Jagd-bombers – that machine-gunned any and all enemy vehicles moving by day, were the nemesis of reconnaissance teams.

D-Day + 13. While the Allied forces struggled to make headway around Caen and Carentan, General Collins' troops reached the west coast of the Cotentin peninsula and were preparing to take Cherbourg.

Arromanches (Gold Beach), 18th June. Eleven days after the arrival of the first Phoenix unit, 115 others had now been sunk offshore in an 8 km-long arc, and formed the breakwater of «Port-Winston», the artificial port so-called in honour of Winston Churchill, whose idea it had been to build it. The three floating pontoons assembled between the 9th and the 18th of June made possible the unloading of 280 ships per day.

... and the capture of Cherbourg

The regular and continued provision of fresh supplies and the availability of numerous means of transport are without doubt essential elements to the success of troops landed in enemy territory. So the Allies needed to control major port facilities to continue advancing in Normandy. This need became all the more pressing on the 20th of June when the storm that had been blowing in the Channel since the day before obliged the Allies to suspend the use of the artificial ports. The one built off Omaha, which was almost totally destroyed, was lost; the British sector port, at Arromanches, was less damaged, but it was not to be back in service until after a month of repairs.

So, when the American 4th, 9th and 79th Infantry converged to the north of Carentan the day after the capture of Barneville, under the command of General Collins, the port of Cherbourg was obviously their main objective. The three divisions advanced northward on a thirty kilometre-wide front, the 4th and the 9th respectively up the east and west coasts, and the 79th in the centre of the peninsula. On the 22nd of June, while massive attacks from the air sapped the morale of the 25,000 Germans defending the harbour town, the three American divisions drove into different parts of the German defensive line, an extensive semi-circle of steel and concrete fortifications built at the same time as the *Atlantikwall* and situated ten kilometres out from the town.

Arromanches, 19th–21st June. For three days the Seine Bay coasts were battered by a violent storm heralding the summer solstice.

Saint-Laurent-sur-Mer (Omaha Beach), 22nd June.
The Allies decided to abandon the construction of the American artificial port at Saint-Laurent-sur-Mer because of the scale of the storm damage there. Many of its units were retrieved and used to repair the port at Arromanches that, although it had been severely damaged, could be rendered serviceable relatively quickly. Thus, by the end of June, 4,000 tonnes of supplies and equipment were once again being offloaded daily.

D-Day + 19. Having reached the west coast of the Cotentin, the Americans made ready to enter Cherbourg. Outside Caen, the Anglo-Canadians were about to begin Operation Epsom to take the Capital of Lower Normandy.

On the 25th of June, fifteen Allied battleships under Admiral Deyo appeared out to sea from the port, escorted by two flotillas of minesweepers. Around midday they set to duelling with the German guns. After three hours of intense bombardment during which the Texas and the Glasgow were hit, the Allies had lost fifty-two men, but had severely damaged the enemy defences.

Although its fate was sealed, the resistance of part of the German garrison was as staunch as it was desperate. For four days, the town was host to a fierce battle. The Americans had to resort to street fighting before they were able to launch the final assault on the arsenal. On the 27th of June, when the arsenal finally fell under Allied control, General von Schlieben and Admiral Hennecke had already surrendered with the main part of the German contingent, in spite of Hitler's repeated orders to fight to the last man. Two days later, the last pockets of resistance were eliminated; on the 30th, the fighting had finished on the rocky moors of the north-western tip of the peninsula, where 6,000 Germans were made prisoner on the Cap de la Hague.

However, the capture of Cherbourg did not prove, at first, to be as beneficial as expected. The port had been so diligently and efficiently sabotaged by the German engineers, that it was to be useless for the best part of a month, and so until the end of July, the beaches and the artificial port at Arromanches, once it had been repaired, continued to be the only routes by which supplies could be brought to the troops in Normandy. Nevertheless, this success allowed General Bradley's army to concentrate its efforts on Saint-Lô, which, by dint of its central position in the heart of the Cotentin, was the road and rail communications crossroads of the region. From this moment on, the «hedgerow warfare» intensified.

Cherbourg, 26th June. Unconcerned by the disarray of the «Eastern Volunteers», the Germans fought everywhere with a ferocity goaded by despair, until their last round was spent.

Cherbourg, 26ᵗʰ June. An American soldier taking down the Todt Organisation sign with help from the town's inhabitants. The organisation, which was responsible for construction work on the Atlantikwall, had set up its head office for the Granville to Trouville-sur-Mer sector in the Hotel Atlantique.

Cherbourg, 27ᵗʰ June. The German garrison counted 25,000 men, mostly older administrative personnel and soldiers; one quarter of the garrison consisted of «Eastern Volunteers».
When his superiors reproached him for having surrendered, General von Sclieben replied with the bitter retort that «one couldn't expect Russians and Poles to fight Americans in France for Germany's benefit.»

Cherbourg, 27th June. As the Allies drew nearer, the Germans undertook the systematic destruction of the port facilities. The harbour was in ruins when the Americans captured it, having been dynamited four days previously, shortly before midnight.

La Haye du Puits, end of June. After capturing Cherbourg, the American 79th and 90th Infantries were given the mission of opening the road to Coutances. The capture of the Haye du Puits was to prove lengthy, difficult and particularly bloody, due to the large number of German troops dug into the hills around the town and abominable weather, which prevented the air force from intervening.
The 79th Infantry only liberated the town on the morning of the 9th of July.

HEDGEROW WARFARE

The American troops, who were obliged to multiply their attacks on the well-hidden German operational bases, were at a disadvantage in the hedgerows, where each of the seemingly endless hedges was another obstacle to the deployment of their armoured units. The Allied strategists had carefully drawn up their battle plan, but had obviously minimised the difficulties of making progress through a labyrinth such as this. The landed troops and tanks, who had little experience of manoeuvres on terrain where visibility was so limited, were sitting ducks for the hidden German gunners and infantry.

Tackling the sunken lanes and the thick hedges of the Manche hedgerows, the Americans attempted to disentangle themselves by attacking the enemy with machine guns and mortars, but they were faced with an enemy who was familiar with the terrain and who put up valiant resistance, and their progress was slow and costly.

Everything changed in mid-July, when General Bradley, who had laughed at the British Funnies, ordered the American tanks to be fitted with «hedge-busters», perfected by Sergeant Culin, and made from the rail tetrahedrons with which Rommel had littered the beaches. This American tank sergeant had welded four steel blades onto the front of his tank, to get through the hedges more easily. Driven hard and fast into a hedge, this equipment opened a breach in the hedges, thus avoiding the tanks' riding up over the mounds of earth and exposing their vulnerable underside, their Achilles' heel, to enemy fire.

2. The reinforced German riposte and the lack of Allied progress, 27th June – 25th July

As Bradley ordered his troops to converge on Saint-Lô, Montgomery multiplied his attacks around Caen. The Anglo-Canadian offensives were aimed at liberating the town, then opening the way southwards to Falaise, but also at keeping the German reserve armoured divisions busy in the sector, in the hope that this would aid American deployment in the Cotentin. But contrary to the hopes of the chief of the 21st Army Group, who expected them in the south, the reinforcement *Panzer* divisions arrived to the north of Caen. Montgomery's troops were thus blocked to the north and west, and he decided to attempt to enter Caen by the south, where there were still no enemy reinforcements.

As soon as the storm on the 19th of June had calmed down, General O'Connor launched Operation Epsom sending three army corps towards the Odon valley. This offensive, a vast movement turning southwards, aimed at permitting the Allies to conquer Caen, still occupied by the Germans twenty days after D-Day.

On the morning of the 26th of June, in fog and heavy rain, 90,000 men 700 tanks and 600 big guns left the north-western periphery of Caen. After two days of fighting during which the Germans had not stopped retreating on a 10 km-wide front, the British captured a bridge over the Odon; the tanks of the 11th Armoured Division immediately took advantage of this event, crossing the river and heading for Caen, following its right bank. General Dollman, chief of the German 7th Army in Normandy, believing the Allied breakthrough to be inevitable, committed suicide in his HQ on the 28th of June on hearing of the fall of Cherbourg.

On the morning of the 29th, however, while it seems the Allied chiefs also believed their victory to be imminent, the British advance was unceremoniously halted at *côte 112*, a small hill dominating the south-west approaches to Caen. The Germans were dug in around this position and defending it resolutely, clinging to the southern slope, which they had managed to hold. Then, with the intervention of the 9th and 10th Panzer divisions, recently transported from the eastern front by road and rail, the fight was taken from the Allies. While young *Waffen SS* covered with explosives threw themselves under British tanks, the powerful German *Tigers* deployed to recapture part of the terrain that had been lost.

On the 30th of June, after having requested the support of the RAF's heavy bombers, which dropped some 1,100 tonnes of bombs on the sector to stop the enemy counter-attack, Montgomery ordered the abandonment of Operation Epsom. He had lost 4,000 men, and decided it

Near Fontenay-le-Pesnel, 26th June. A Sherman tank belonging to the British 49th Infantry, engaged in Operation Epsom, exploding on the verge of the road from Caen to Villers-Bocage, having been hit by an enemy mortar shell.
The Germans mocked the American-built tanks, so much more vulnerable than their own, nicknaming them «Tommy's cooker». The British, who were no less aware of the fact, called them «Ronsons» after the lighters, for which the advertisements claimed that they would always «light first time».

Outskirts of Caen. The 9th and 10th Panzers, which had distinguished themselves in April on the Eastern Front, where they had halted the Soviet offensive at Tarnopol, were dispatched to Normandy. General Hauser's men, who arrived on the 23rd of June, repeated their feat of arms at Esquay-Notre-Dame opposite the Anglo-Canadians; their decisive intervention rang the knell of the third Allied attempt to take Caen.

Beginning of July. The capture of Caen, D-Day's unattained objective, became a focus for the strategic disagreements between Bradley and Montgomery. The former was exasperated by the cheerful enthusiasm of the latter, sharing the pessimism of those, ever more numerous, who feared that the front would one day be pierced, and who were wary of winter catching the Allies still in Normandy. The modifications wrought by Montgomery after the failure of Operation Epsom were as much a consequence of the criticism aimed at him as the fruit of his dread of seeing the fighting for Caen transformed into a war of position, reminiscent of the Great War.

would be prudent to heed the advice of General O'Connor, who suggested that the units that had crossed the Odon should retrace their steps.

The third attempt to take Caen was also a costly failure resulting in minimal territorial gains. In total, after three weeks of combat the Anglo-Canadian positions had barely changed since the evening of D-Day: the Germans were still in possession of Caen and the villages to the north and west, which they had transformed into veritable fortified positions. Although it was a tactical failure, Operation Epsom was not totally without effect. By preventing the reinforcements from reaching the Cotentin, it facilitated the American deployment, alleviating the serious difficulties the Americans were encountering in extracting themselves from the hedgerows.

When the attempted outflanking on the west finally failed at the bottom of *côte 112,* Montgomery resolved to attack the town head on, a tactic he had hitherto refused to consider, wishing to avoid a massacre. This change of strategy also made new tactical options attractive. In order to gain territory, the infantry's attempted breakthroughs, which had had armoured support hitherto, would from now on be systematically preceded by heavy bombers, whose mission would be to weaken the German defences by methodical bombardments.

Operations Windsor and Charnwood, and the liberation of Carpiquet and Caen (4th - 9th July)

From the 4th of July on, the Allies went back on the offensive with the launch of operation Windsor, north-west of Caen. Strongly supported by tanks, 5,000 men of the Canadian 3rd Infantry attacked the Carpiquet aerodrome once again.

Once more they suffered heavy losses, but finally succeeded in taking it after four days of furious conflagration, during which the young recruits of the 12th *SS Panzer Hitlerjugend* would run from their bunkers, clutching grenades, to disable the Allied tanks and mortars. In order to overcome this particularly fierce resistance, some positions were only taken with the use of Crocodiles, the 79th Armoured Division's flame-throwing tanks.

Caen, 8th July. During the morning, while rescuers were busy in the ruins of the Place des Petites Boucheries, the Panzer tanks of the 12th Panzer SS left the northern half of the city, heading towards the centre and over the Orne, to take up position on the right bank.

Caen, 9ᵗʰ July, 1 p.m. After 33 days of hard fighting, the Allies broke through into the city. The British press spoke of the taking of Caen, celebrating the event as a major victory somewhat earlier than events on the ground warranted.

To diminish the impatience rife in public opinion as much as to quieten the criticism levelled at Montgomery, this photo of Canadians of the 9ᵗʰ Brigade posing at the western entry to Caen was widely shown over the following days.

Caen, 9ᵗʰ July, 3 p.m. The British 3ʳᵈ Infantry meeting up with the men of the Canadian 9ᵗʰ Brigade on the Place Saint-Pierre.
A British anti-tank gun lying in ambush in the Vaugueux area of town, at the bottom of the Rue des Chanoines, in case of an enemy counter-attack.

Caen, 10th July. A British army tank crew struggling through the ruins of the Moulin-au-Roy district. In the Rue Saint-Pierre, a reconnaissance patrol having the same difficulties, all the more so as the destroyed buildings made excellent bases for the occupying troops.
Allied soldiers now had to scour the ruins to oust the Germans dug into them.

At dawn on the 8th of July, Operation Charnwood was launched against Caen. British and Canadian troops penetrated the western, northern and eastern approaches to the town in force, after 500 RAF heavy bombers had dropped 2,500 tonnes of bombs on the north of the town. But in spite of massive artillery support, the 115,000 men committed to the operation progressed slowly and laboriously.

In fact, although it had made it possible for the three divisions to advance into the town, the preliminary intervention of the British aviation, albeit effective, proved quickly to have caused problems for their deployment *intra muros*: the tanks could not act freely because of the rubble strewn over the main thoroughfares and the infantry was obliged to fight for each street, the piles of rubble offering the occupying troops all sorts of protection.

After 36 hours of fierce fighting, the Anglo-Canadians had succeeded in taking the northern and western quarters of Caen, but had not managed to cross the Orne, the Germans having destroyed the bridges across it. The latter had withdrawn to the right bank of the river that runs through the town, where they had established a solid defensive line, making it possible for them to hold the southern and eastern quarters. In order to seize the south and east and totally liberate the town, the Allies only solution was a fourth offensive.

Caen, 11ᵗʰ July. Living under the exchanges of fire between Allies and Germans, bombarding each other's positions across the Orne, the people of Caen left the town, nervously exhausted.

CAEN BOMBARDED, MUTILATED, YET ALIVE

Had all gone as planned, Caen should have been liberated, intact, on the 6th of June. Liberated it was, but in ruins and 43 days behind schedule, after weeks of siege and bombardments.

It had become the symbol of German resistance in Normandy on the very evening of D-Day, and so was prey to the very many heavy bombers that Montgomery eventually sent in to secure victory.

After the first bombardments of the 6th of June, between ten and fifteen thousand of Caen's homeless inhabitants were lodged in the buildings of the Lycée Malherbe – now the town hall – and the Bon-Sauveur, under the vaults of the Abbaye-aux-Hommes or in the Eglise Saint-Etienne. Others hastily left their homes for the shelter of the local quarries and mushroom-growing caves, taking what they could with them.

For weeks, these people improvised a community. They surpassed themselves in their efforts to find ways of lessening the extreme precarity of their shared situation.

Outskirts of Saint-Lô, mid-July. In order to hamper
the Allies' progress, the Germans, who knew the area
well, made effective use of all the opportunities for
ambush offered by the hedgerows.

The belated and difficult liberation
of Saint-Lô and Caen

While the men of the British 2nd Army made difficult headway in Caen, their colleagues of the American 1st Army were experiencing similar problems in the Cotentin. Two weeks after the capture of Cherbourg, they were experiencing severe difficulties in progressing through the hedgerows. They were pushing forward a front 45 km wide, and had lost 10,000 men dead or wounded for a mere 10 km gained, and had not yet succeeded in taking Saint-Lô, an objective whose accomplishment SHAEF had forecast for D-Day +10. In spite of their efforts and the loss of 1,200 men since mid-June, the 2nd Infantry had still not managed to take possession of the few kilometres between them and the *préfecture* (the main city) of the Manche department.

Thus it was that on the 11th of July, General Bradley decided to engage the services of the 29th and 35th Infantries to launch a large scale offensive on the town. On the afternoon of the 18th, after a week of artillery barrage and aerial bombardments, the vanguard of the 29th Infantry managed to thread its way to the centre of a town that was no more than a collection of ruins. Having lost 2,000 men in this attack alone, it took the three divisions a further week to eliminate the resisting German units isolated round Saint-Lô.

In Caen, where the left bank was by now under Allied control, the Anglo-Canadians launched operation Goodwood on the 18th of July. This fourth offensive was more than a plan to simply complete the liberation of the town. General Dempsey, whose had masterminded it, envisaged deploying the British 2nd Army's tanks right across the plain to the east of Caen, bringing them over the Bourgébus ridge and, beyond it, regrouping to continue advancing southwards towards Falaise.

Outskirts of Saint-Lô, mid-July. The Germans, who did not have enough tanks, fell back on the use of anti-tank weapons. The American tank and armoured vehicles' crews dreaded the Panzerschreck (left) and the Panzerfaust bazookas (right).

Saint-Lô, 18ᵗʰ July. The final signpost before the town, and the last few moments of freedom for this defeated German soldier.

Saint-Lô, 18ᵗʰ July. The destruction was so absolute
that the convoys that entered it could barely
distinguish the roads formerly criss-crossing the town.
There was so much rubble that the course of the
Dollée, here on the right, was diverted.

Caen, 18th July. The Anglo-Canadians were still striving to conquer the right bank, ten days after having taken the northern half of the town.

At 5h30 the RAF and the US Air Force went into action. 2,000 heavy bombers flew over the southern periphery of Caen and dropped some 5,600 tonnes of bombs in under an hour. The bombardment was so intense that Caen plain was shrouded in a thick cloud of dust and smoke. The German tanks on site were literally flipped upside down. When the aviation had finished, 1,000 field guns opened fire on the town's right bank and the surrounding countryside. Finally, around 8 o'clock, 75,000 men, divided into eight divisions and with support from 700 tanks, entered the fray. For the first few hours, they progressed rapidly. The Germans, who had still been in position on the right bank that morning, abandoned it to the Allies, driven out by the sheer torrential weight of fiery steel that threatened to engulf them. At the same moment, the biggest embroilment of tanks during the battle of Normandy was taking place in the plain to the east of the town. At first, the British looked like coming through this battle victorious; Cagny, 6 km south of Caen, was captured during the evening.

On the morning of the 19th, the Canadians of General Simonds' 22nd Army Corps entered the southern areas of Caen, crossing bridges they had spent the night building. The town, which had been fought over, and in, since D-Day, was finally liberated at the end of the afternoon, forty-three days after the date initially anticipated. Further south, in the Cagny sector, enthusiasm was giving way to disappointment. The Germans had rallied and were defending Bourguébus, close by, which controlled the road to Falaise. The Allies lost over one hundred tanks in a few hours, at the hands of the anti-tank guns and Tigers of the 1st and 12th Panzer SS. The next day, torrential rain turned the Caen plain into a mud bath, in which the tanks became particularly vulnerable targets, with drastically reduced mobility. The British, bogged down and brutally beaten below the Bourguébus ridge, renounced the pursuit of their offensive, preferring to defend the positions they had paid for so dearly; operation Goodwood was over.

At the time, this fourth Anglo-Canadian offensive in under a month was considered a partial failure, its results being a far cry from the Allies' declared ambitions, in spite of the forces involved. In three days of fighting the British 2nd Army had lost 6,000 men and 400 tanks (four times more than the Germans) for relatively small territorial gains. However, outwith the satisfaction and the relief of having liberated Caen at last, they had also obliged the enemy to concentrate their forces in the sector, once again preventing them from sending reserve units to the Cotentin, where General Bradley, flush with his success in Saint-Lô, could allow himself some optimism as he considered a new offensive aimed at moving his troops out of the Manche hedgerows, to which tank warfare was so badly adapted.

Caen, 18th July. A bombardment, the like of which had hitherto not been seen, smashed the German defensive lines in position on the plain south of Caen to smithereens: 2,200 bombers dropped 7,000 tonnes of bombs on the sector. The bombardment was such, that a number of the enemy's tanks were literally flipped upside down. Operation Goodwood was launched.

Caen, 19th July. Early in the morning, the first Canadian troops crossed the Orne. With the help of the FFI of the Fred Scaramoni company, the Canadians managed to force the Germans out of the town. 80% of it destroyed, with hundreds of wounded, and mourning its 2,000 dead, Caen was liberated at last.

Cagny, 20th July. After the liberation of Caen, the Anglo-Canadians took up the pursuit of Germans who had retreated south of the city. Cagny, theatre of a violent clash between Tiger and Sherman tanks, was liberated after fighting right in the centre of the village.

Vaucelles, 23rd - 27th July. The Canadian 7th Artillery Regiment shelled the Bourgebus ridge from the suburbs of Caen, in support of the British 7th Armour's tanks, which were attempting to dislodge those of the 1st and 12th *Panzer SS.*

Caen, end of July. While some units headed for the front line to fight in the hope of gaining a little more territory, others rested behind the lines for a few hours, before heading back to the front to relieve their companions in the fray.
Canadians drinking tea in front of a house where soldiers of the Wehrmacht had been billeted during the occupation of Caen...

... and British soldiers taking the chance to rid
themselves of the smoke and the dust of battle.

159

3. Allied breakthroughs and the German retreat, 25th July–21st August

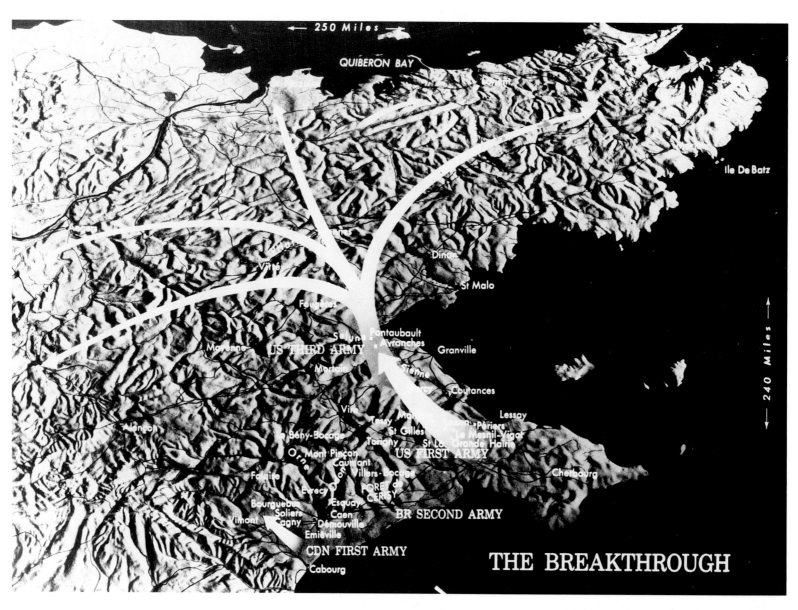

THE BREAKTHROUGH

Operation Cobra. The American offensive, a southward push down the Cotentin to finish with the exhausting «hedgerow warfare», which had been in preparation since mid-July, was postponed from the 20th until the 25th of July, due to bad weather preventing the preliminary intervention of the air force.

The capture of Saint-Lô broke the deadlock in the American sector, and the taking of Caen gave renewed impetus to the Anglo-Canadians. The liberating armies launched into large-scale offensives, relieved that the battle had not degenerated into stalemate and a war of position. At first, these offensives were designed to force results, but they soon came to be seen as a means to surrounding the German army in Normandy, an idea which grew progressively on the Allied military chiefs.

Operation Cobra, or the American breakthrough in the Cotentin

On the 25th of July, while the Anglo-Canadians were having difficulty forcing their way through to Falaise, the Americans, who were by now in control of the area around Saint-Lô, headed for the south of the Cotentin. Operation Cobra was under way. Preceded by the habitual powerful aerial preparation, the Allied offensive was fast and effective.

The *Division Lehr,* dug in a few kilometres south of Saint-Lô, was severely weakened by the loss of a sizeable number of its tanks, rendered useless by the Allied air raids in the Saint-Gilles sector. As soon as the bombardments had finished, the men of the American 1st Army poured into the breach thus created in the German defensive lines. The progress of the GIs was slow to begin with, but accelerated as the days went by; for all their dogged determination, the grenadiers of the *Division Lehr* were unable to resist the sheer power of the forces they were up against. Thanks to the use of the «Rhinoceros», a hedge-busting tank newly invented by an American under-officer, General Collins' divisions tore the resisting German positions apart. The Germans, who were weakened, disorientated and sometimes completely surrounded as they were in Roncey, yielded territory every day. On the 29th, the tanks of the US Army's 4th Armoured Division liberated Coutances; on the 31st, they entered Avranches and Ducey, to the south east, while the 6th Armoured Division followed suite in Granville.

Seven weeks after D-Day, the Americans were ready to move into Brittany and a reorganisation of the Allied forces on the Norman front was undertaken. This reorganisation, scheduled for when the Cotentin breakthrough was to have been achieved, regrouped the 1st and 3rd Armies, respectively commanded by Generals Hodges and Patton, in the American 12th Army Corps, placed under the orders of General Bradley. Montgomery remained in charge of the Allied 21st Army Corps, with General Dempsey's British 2nd Army in charge of the centre of the front, and General Crerar's Canadian 1st Army on the eastern front.

Patton's divisions took advantage of the breach south of Avranches to liberate Pontaubault on the 1st of August. They crossed the Couesnon and fanned out: some, belonging to the 8th Army Corps, headed for Saint-Malô and Rennes; the others, of the 15th Corps, began the wide circle which was to take them, via Fougères, Laval and Le Mans to Paris. The war of attrition in the Normandy hedgerows was succeeded by mobile warfare, which the tank divisions had been looking forward to for so long. Their newly recovered freedom of movement meant they could be put to full use on the battlefield, and play a decisive role in battle.

The fruit of the imagination of Sergeant Curtis Culin Jr., welded to the front of two-thirds of the tanks engaged in Operation Cobra, was unarguably a decisive factor in the speed of the American breakthrough in the Cotentin.

Deprived of all air support, the German ground forces were reduced to hoping for the worst weather possible, which would buy them a little time, in the hope that the order to retreat would come before the disaster that was rapidly becoming inevitable with the passing weeks. The noticeable absence of the Luftwaffe in the Norman skies left them dreading the days of clement weather, which would give the Allies' pilots the opportunity of launching devastating air raids on their positions. «When you see a white plane, it's an American; a black one, it's the RAF. If you don't see anything, it's the Luftwaffe!» This joke, which did the rounds of the Flak gunners, was a clear indication of the bitterness felt in the Wehrmacht's ranks.

Outskirts of La Chapelle-Enjuger, 25th July. Operation Cobra began with an aerial bombardment of stunning violence: 1,500 heavy bombers dropped 3,750 tonnes of incendiary bombs on a sector 6 km long by 2 km wide, following which General Collins engaged the American 2nd and 3rd Armoured Divisions in the breach created between Marigny and Saint-Gilles.

Coutances, 28th July. Through the smoke from the artillery, stretcher-beareres from the US Army Medical Corps evacuating a man from a reconnaissance unit of the American 4th Armour, whose vehicle had run over a mine at the town gates.

Leaving Coutances, 29th July. After liberating the town, the Americans headed down the road to Avranches.

165

Roncey, 29th July. Having rapidly fled the episcopal city, the 2nd and 17th Panzer SS found themselves surrounded south-east of Coutances. Cornered in the Roncey sector, and subjected to an aerial bombardment that lasted for six hours, some 7,000 Germans surrendered, having run out of ammunition.

For their part, General Hodges' men forced the enemy back along a line from Mortain to Vire, in order to cover this deployment, which was vulnerable to a reaction from the *Wehrmacht,* because of the narrowness of the breach in the German lines. They too sought to force a passage through enemy defences, in their case towards Vire, in the hope of linking up with the British, who had launched Operation Bluecoat on the 30th of July, with this same intention.

While the Americans were preparing to achieve a spectacular breakthrough, Montgomery launched his offensive between Villers-Bocage and Vire. This attack was entrusted to General Dempsey's 2nd Army, and was designed to help the deployment of Patton's divisions and also to give the Canadian 1st Army the time it needed to regroup. The Canadians had been strongly countered a few days earlier during operation Spring, and were to renew their attempts to advance on Falaise. The Canadian attack began on the 25th of July and ended the same day, due to their absolute lack of progress and the severe losses suffered after the few hours of combat during which 500 soldiers died and twice as many were wounded.

On the other hand, the British attack was more conclusive. It was led by General O'Connor's 8th Corps, and resulted in territorial gains of some thirty kilometres towards Vire and Aunay-sur-Odon, and Villers-Bocage, which had been abandoned on the disastrous 13th of June, was captured on the 4th, followed on the 6th by Mont Pinçon, a strategic point whose peak rises 354 m above sea-level, after an assault that finished with hand-to-hand fighting.

So, at the beginning of August, the breakthrough on the western front was confirmed, with the capture of Mortain by the American 1st Infantry on the 3rd, then Vire on the 8th, by the 29th Infantry, who lost 1,000 men while covering the thirty kilometres separating the two towns. In the centre, the Allied advance became more pronounced, in spite of the difficulties encountered by the British, who were once again confronted with the formidable 9th and 10th *SS Panzer,* which had hurried back up from the banks of the Odon. Only on the eastern front did there seem to be a stalemate since the taking of Caen. The Germans were dug into the galleries of the vast mining complex stretching south of the town, where they were sheltered from the aerial and artillery bombardments and used the existing network of tunnels to dispatch troops to sectors under attack.

Consequently, two months after D-Day, the Canadians were still unable to break through to Falaise, in the hands of the 1st *SS Panzer.*

Avranches, 31st July. The American 4th Armour liberating the town. The Americans, who had advanced 60 km and taken 20,000 prisoners in five days, were preparing to leave the Cotentin, on the point of achieving their breakthrough.

Utah Beach, 1st of August. Forty-nine months after having secretly «left France with rage in my heart, but unvanquished nonetheless», to present himself to General de Gaulle in London, the ex-Captain de Hautecloque once more set foot on French soil. Having taken an assumed name so that his family, which had stayed in France, would not be worried by his involvement with the leader of the Free French, he distinguished himself fighting with the Allies in North Africa.

Leading a hundred men, he captured the fortress at Koufra in March 1941, which feat won him his first General's stars. Then, participating in both Fezzan campaigns, he linked up with Montgomery's British 8th Army in January 1943, in Tripoli. Straight after that, he engaged in the Tunisian campaign, with his troops re-baptised «Force L», and defeated the 90th Panzer in March, at Ksar Rhilane.

168

Utah Beach, 1st August. Created in North Africa by General Leclerc during the summer of 1943, the French 2nd Armour counted 16,000 men, 3,000 armoured vehicles and 250 Sherman tanks. It landed in Saint-Martin de Varreville, after being transferred to England in May 1944.

It was incorporated into General Patton's 3rd US Army's 15th Army Corps and went straight to the breach at Avranches to join the eastwards movement.

Cahagnes, 2nd August. A tank of the British
7th Armour heading for Aunay-sur-Odon across
the destroyed village square, deserted by all except
an abandoned horse.

Above: **Aunay-sur-Odon, 5th August 1944.** The British 7th Armour liberated this village, at the edge of the hedgerow country around Vire. However, as it was considered to be one of the possible springboards for a German counter-offensive, Aunay was totally wiped off the map, as of the 15th of June. «Aunay was here...», read one sign.

Opposite: **Aunay-sur-Odon, 1938.**

Operation Lüttich, the first and last major German offensive in Normandy

Faced with the success of Operation Cobra, many German commanders were considering retreating to the other side of the Seine, to avoid being surrounded, a risk that was becoming more imminent by the day around the positions held by the 7th Army. Be that as it may, 2,000 kilometres away in Germany, Hitler decided the opposite, now convinced by the General Patton's appearance in Normandy that there would not be any other Allied invasion, and that the invasion on the 6th of June was not merely a diversionary tactic. Rather than shaking his confidence in the confrontation's outcome, his new convictions decided him to throw all available reserves on site into the battle in the Cotentin, while dispatching reserves to Normandy.

Hitler attributed the *Wehrmacht's* numerous reversals of fortune since 1942 to the anti-nazi generals who had plotted the assassination attempt against him on the 20th of July. He was persuaded that their elimination at the hands of the Gestapo would herald the return of the heady victories of 1940-41. He rejected the idea of retreating, even for strategic reasons, and ordered Field-marshal von Kluge, who had replaced von Rundstedt on the 2nd of July, after the latter had been heard to make defeatist comments, to launch Operation *Lüttich*. The counter-attack was intended to force the eastbound divisions of the American 3rd Army to retreat, and close the breach they had opened south east of Avranches.

During the night of 6th-7th August seven divisions, including four of the 7th Army's *Panzer*, under the command of the SS General Hausser since the death of General Dollman, set out to tackle the American troops. They attacked head on in the sector between Vire and Mortain, with 250 tanks and 32 big guns.

Their vanguard managed to slip between the Allies' positions and penetrate 10 km behind Allied lines, isolating several American battalions. The notorious 2nd *SS Panzer «Das Reich»*, famous since its recovery of Montauban where it had been on the 6th of June, took advantage of the morning fog to capture Mortain, then headed for Saint-Hilaire-du-Harcouët to put a stop to the continuous procession of Allied troops south east of Avranches. They left Mortain, but were brought up short by an isolated and surrounded battalion of the American 30th Infantry, who were defending the rocky slopes of a promontory going by the name of *côte 317*.

From the middle of the afternoon on, the German counter-attack marked time. Shortly after the fog had lifted, the Allied aviation had entered the fray and changed the course of events: for eight hours, the US Air Force Typhoons hunted down the German tanks and destroyed them with incendiary rockets. By nightfall, the Germans still held the town, but only had thirty or so tanks left. Operation *Lüttich* was a fiasco from the outset, lacking men, sufficient equipment and air support. Nevertheless, Kluge pursued the battle, as the Führer had formally charged him to maintain control of the terrain.

Marshal von Kluge, appointed commander of the armies on the Western Front on the 2nd of July, was considered to be one of the Wehrmacht's anti-tank warfare specialists.
He launched Operation Lüttich on the 6th of August, filled with consternation, but respectful of orders from Hitler, but the German counter-attack was more of a last desperate spurt of effort than an offensive with any serious chance of stopping the 3rd US Army's tanks, bumper to bumper in the narrow, week-old breach south-east of Avranches.

Mortain, 7th August. After having recaptured the town early in the morning, the men of the 2nd Panzer SS «Das Reich» were driven out again that very afternoon, following violent, sometimes hand-to-hand, fighting. On the evening of the first day of the offensive, Marshal von Kluge could but accept the obvious: Operation Lüttich was a fiasco that heralded another, much greater disaster.

During Operation Lüttich, the recruits of the SS divisions proved themselves hardy combatants. Only when the order came did they relinquish their grip on the Mortain salient.

The fighting in the « Falaise pocket », and the outcome of the Battle of Normandy

The German defences south of Caen had been stretched to allow the counter-attack in the Avranches sector, and Montgomery hoped to take advantage of this situation. On the 8th of August, he launched operation Totalize in the hope of quickly capturing Falaise, a mission entrusted to the General Simonds' Canadian 2nd Army Corps, incorporating General Maczek's Polish 1st Armoured Division, which had landed at Courseulles and Arromanches the previous week.

The offensive was launched on the 26th anniversary of the massive Canadian offensive on the German army at Amiens during the Great War, which had heralded the defeat of Imperial Germany, but was less incisive than had been anticipated. The 12th *SS Panzer* reservists defended their positions with ferocity. Battle-hardened by weeks of combat around Caen, they inflicted heavy losses on the Allied troops and contained their offensive 10 km north of Falaise. Consequently, Allied command dispatched the 3rd US Army's 15th Army Corps, which had liberated Le Mans on the 8th of August, in the direction of the Canadian 1st Army the next day, in order to win a rapid and decisive victory and seize the chance of surrounding the German army in Normandy.

Field-marshal von Kluge noticed this manoeuvre on the 11th of August, and asked Hitler for permission to abandon the counter-offensive at Mortain, and to begin organising the withdrawal of the 150,000 men still in position in Normandy, but Hitler refused. Moreover, he repeated his orders to maintain pressure on Avranches, and demanded that the Germans attack at Argentan and Falaise too, to prevent the American-Canadian pincer movement from closing its jaws.

Judging the Führer's orders impossible to execute, taking into account the scattered positions of the troops, their fatigue, and lack of adequate equipment, von Kluge overrode Hitler's orders and enjoined the German troops to evacuate the Mortain extrusion. Hitler was furious and relieved him of his command. He was replaced by Field-marshal Model, a veteran of similarly difficult situations on the eastern front. However, the withdrawal continued in many places, but in disorderly haste due to having been undertaken belatedly, and as a consequence of the Allies' rapid progress.

Following the liberation of Alençon on the morning of the 12th, the columns of the 3rd US Army, including General Leclerc's 2nd Armoured Division, reached the gates of Argentan that same evening. 32 km further north, General Simonds' 2nd Army Corps launched operation Tractable on the 14th of August. Two days later, after another taxing offensive, the Canadian 2nd Infantry entered Falaise, where the last die-hard men of the 12th *Panzer Hitlerjugend* lay in ambush. For 24 hours they fought in the streets, until the last of them had fallen. During this time, the rest of the Canadians and the Polish 1st Armour moved forward on both sides of the town, reducing the distance separating them from the Americans of the 3rd Army by a further 10 km.

Alençon, 12th August. The crew of the half-track «Picrocole» of General Leclerc's 2nd Armour going through the town, acclaimed by the inhabitants it met. This was the only French division involved in the Battle of Normandy. It joined the fray south of Avranches, liberating Saint-James on the 7th of August. It was involved in the great movement that left the German armies surrounded, and then in the fighting to liberate Le Mans and Alençon, before the bitter fighting in the Ecouves forest on the way to Ecouché. Dispatched in support of the Americans of the 90th Infantry, one of its units participated in the closing of the Falaise pocket.

Amblie, 7th August. General Maczek giving his last instructions to the officers of the units leaving on operations in the field HQ of the Polish 1st Armoured Division.
Having landed in Courseulles and Arromanches on the 31st of July, the Polish division was integrated into General Simonds' 2nd Canadian Army Corps.
It counted 15,000 men and 380 tanks and participated in Operations Totalize and Tractable, under the command of general Maczek, a veteran of the campaigns in Poland in September 1939 and in France in May-June 1940.
Spearheading the British 2nd Army's advance on Falaise, the Polish played a decisive role in the constitution and subsequent closing of the Falaise pocket.

Argentan 13th August. Bradley and Montgomery had planned to surround the German 7th Army, drawing the net tight at Argentan. But the failure of Totalize had hindered the British 11th Armour, charged with taking the town. So as not to upset Montgomery, Bradley halted the 3rd Army, obliging the French 2nd Armour and the American 5th Armour to camp at the gates of Argentan, while the 116th Panzer clung to the ruins in an attempt to prevent the Germans being completely surrounded.

Falaise, 17th August. The German 1st SS Armoured Army Corps left the town to regroup near Vimoutiers and the Canadians captured it, but William the Conqueror's native town was only liberated in its entirety the next morning.

Falaise 17th August. It took the Canadian 2nd Infantry, advancing street by street, over a day to silence the remaining pockets of German resistance, notably sixty-odd SS from the «Hitlerjugend» division, who had chosen to act on the Führer's call to «die fighting, rather than give so much as an inch of ground». They had regrouped inside the Ecole supérieure for the showdown with the Allies. When the Canadians captured their position on the morning of the 18th, they only found four survivors, all wounded.

From then on, with the Canadians and the Polish to the north, the British to the west, and the Americans in the south, the vice closed slowly but surely on the German units in the Falaise sector. Amongst them, many of the officers and soldiers who had been on the front line without respite since D-Day were nervously exhausted by the incessant Allied bombardments, and just wanted to get out of Normandy, where the spectre of defeat, and with it captivity for the lucky ones, loomed large. Only the SS, blinded by their attachment and unswerving loyalty to the Führer, refused to face the facts.

When Field-marshal Model arrived in his headquarters in Saint-Germain-en-Laye on the 17th of August, he quickly realised there was no solution other than pursuing the retreat initiated by his predecessor. When Hitler was informed, he gave his consent for the troops to be brought east of the Dives. During the night of the 17th-18th the bulk of the German forces crossed the river between Trun and Chambois. To allow a maximum number of men to escape from «der Kessel von Falaise», Model decided to dispatch two *Panzer* divisions ahead of the Canadians and Americans, before their inevitable and imminent link-up. As it was, the Canadian 4th Armour took Trun and Saint-Pierre-sur-Dives on the morning of the 18th. A detachment of the Polish 1st Armour took up position on Mont-Ormel, which dominates the whole of the Dives valley, while a second Polish group completed the encircling of the Falaise pocket, linking up with a regiment of the American 90th Infantry at Chambois, a small village situated on the main road running down the valley.

Although it was closed around 50,000 trapped Germans, the Falaise pocket was not completely sealed off straight away. Struggling to escape with energy fed by despair, the cornered Germans attempted to smash their way through the Allied lines. Furious fighting, sometimes hand-to-hand broke out around Trun, Saint-Lambert, Chambois and Coudehard, transforming the area into an «infernal cauldron». On the 20th of August, thanks to an attack from the exterior against the 1,800 Poles in position on Mont-Ormel since the day before, elements of the 2nd and 9th SS Panzer managed to create a breach, allowing several thousand men to escape, among their number Generals Hausser, chief of the German 7th Army and von Lüttwitz, commander of the 2nd *Panzer,* both severely wounded during the operation, and General Meindl, chief of the German 2nd Parachute Regiment.

But the next day, when the Canadians of the 4th Armoured Division met up with the Poles isolated on Mont-Ormel, all escape routes were solidly barred; the Falaise pocket was rendered impenetrable through the heroic resistance of General Maczek's men. At that moment, the German soldiers' fate was sealed. Caught in a net, without munitions, they stopped fighting and surrendered. On the evening of the 21st of August, the carnage was over. Although many aspects of the battle in the Falaise pocket resembled the struggle in Stalingrad and its outcome, the confrontation was not «Normandy's Stalingrad» as has often been said and written. Even if 10,000 Germans died attempting to escape the trap that surrounded them, and 40,000 others were obliged to surrender, the majority of the German troops in Normandy managed to avoid sharing their fate.

Falaise Pocket, 17th August. The German eastward retreat was now well under way. Since the previous evening, there had been a rush to escape before they were completely surrounded. «Every man for himself» seemed to be the general rule in the scramble to escape. Some managed to slip through the Allied lines discreetly.

Falaise Pocket, 17th August. Who knows what fate reserved for this officer, who, having escaped unscathed from the machine gunning of his car, but in shock, continued on foot?

«Death Row», 21st August. The wrecks and debris
lining the roads and tracks for kilometres give some
idea of the last battle in the Falaise pocket.

«Death Row», 21st August. In a stampede, thousands of surrounded Germans attempted to flee along the small road from Moissy to Coudehard, where the 2nd *Korps SS Panzer* had opened a passage by counter-attacking from the exterior, but the Allied air forces intervened en masse to destroy the German columns under a hail of blazing steel.

«Death Row», 21st August. Many Germans who refused
to surrender tried to force their way out. Although
a large number of them managed to escape, there were
also many who could not get through, pinned down
under Allied fire.

Saint-Lambert-sur-Dives, 21st August. The carnage came
to an end with the last surrenders. Within the Falaise
pocket, thousands of human corpses lay beside those
of animals and the wrecks of all sorts of vehicles.
Eisenhower, who went there on the 23rd of August,
reported that «it was possible to walk for hundreds of
metres, walking only on decomposing human remains,
in a heavy silence, in a luxuriant countryside where
all life had brutally ceased».

Saint-Lambert-sur-Dives, 19th August. German soldiers, completely surrounded, surrendering to Major Currie's men (Canadian 4th Armour), watched by a cameraman from the Canadian ground forces' film crew, who was filming the scene.

Falaise Pocket, 22nd August. Prisoners, most of them very young, faces drawn, some smiling, some bitter, waiting to be informed of their next destination. Many certainly regretted having been obliged to surrender, but all were relieved to get out of the «Kessel von Falaise» alive and, moreover, unharmed. The war was not over for them, but the prospect of captivity must have seemed like gentle penitence compared to the hell they had just lived through.

... from the «Falaise pocket» to Berchtesgaden

After two and a half months of relentless fighting, the last surrenders in Tournai-sur-Odon drew what is now called the battle of Normandy to a close. The confrontation that began before daybreak on the 6th of June on the shores of the Seine Bay ended on the 21st of August after an almighty bloodbath inland, not far from Falaise. Two million men and women, including military nursing staff, five hundred thousand vehicles and three million tonnes of equipment, goods and munitions were necessary to triumph over an enemy who, in spite of the circumstances, put up a stout and fierce resistance.

This victory, which opened the way to Paris, and beyond, to Germany, fifteen days ahead of General Eisenhower's predictions (D-Day + 75 and not D-Day + 90), was obtained at great cost. During ten weeks of combat, 40,000 Allied soldiers had perished and 200,000 had been wounded; some, in both cases, were victims of mistakes, having been bombed by their own aviation. Nearly 16,000 others were finally declared missing; among their number were the many aviators shot down over Normandy.

Such was the price of victory in Normandy. Defeat for the *Wehrmacht* and its auxiliary units was no cheaper. The German forces had not been able to avoid disaster, completely losing 25 out of the 38 divisions involved in the battle; among the surviving units, some were reduced to a tenth of their initial size. A total of 55,000 men were killed, 140,000 wounded and 200,000 more taken prisoner. Thus diminished, and abandoning 1,500 tanks, 2,000 field guns and 20,000 vehicles on site, the German army jeopardised its chances of making a successful retreat, which it began in a panic and pursued in confusion. In short, the battle of Normandy was the most consequential defeat inflicted on the Germans since Stalingrad, eighteen months previously.

Three days after the Falaise pocket was definitively sewn up, the Americans of the 3rd Army were on the Seine; General Leclerc's tanks were poised to enter Paris. Nothing and no one seemed capable of stopping the Allies' eastward progress. They took advantage of the collapse of the Normandy front, continuing to drive back the remains of the routed German army in Normandy. For the *Wehrmacht*, confronted with the landing of Allied troops in Provence from the 15th of August, the final defeat now seemed inevitable, given the extent to which the twelve week struggle on the beaches and in the Norman countryside had wiped out its finest units, which had been dispatched as reinforcements to repel the invaders.

These mortal blows inflicted on the German army on the western front, the landings on the 6th of June 1944 and the battle of Normandy, were obviously decisive phases in the Second World War. However, the victory of the invading troops did not bring an end to the conflict. It was to be over eight months of fighting later that the Allies finally secured the capitulation of Germany.

In Normandy, the landing operation went on until January 1945. Between times, on the 24th of December 1944, the Allies suffered a last German attack. That evening, as watch-night services were being sung, the Léopoldville, requisitioned for the transport of British troops, was fired

at by a German submarine cruising off Cherbourg. The liner was hit by a torpedo and sank in a matter of minutes with 1,700 men on board.

The liberating and occupying troops were now fighting further afield, and the noise of battle moved away from Normandy and the bombers deserted its sky. Only rumours now filtered back to the Normans, who set about resuscitating their region, devastated by the unprecedented violence of the conflict.

Very few towns and villages were unscathed. Caen, Saint-Lô, Vire, Coutances, Falaise, Argentan, Sées were disfigured beyond recognition; some hamlets had disappeared entirely. In the streets, lined with rubble and ruined by tracked vehicles, the residual stink of charred flesh mingled with the smell of ash. On the coast, the multiple bomb impacts had given the landscape a lunar aspect in many places. In the countryside, the fields had been churned up by the tanks' manoeuvres, the hedges gutted and the trees toppled.

As for the civilian victims, it was impossible to count them with anything like accuracy. Today, thanks to recent research, we know that 19,000 of the men, women and children of Normandy perished during the battle that was to precipitate the defeat of the *Wehrmacht,* and with it the fall of the 3rd German Reich.

Caen, rue de la Délivrande. Monument to the memory of the civilian victims of the liberation bombardments.

THE NORMANS AND THEIR LIBERATORS

Contrary to the expectations of the Allied military chiefs, who were worried before D-Day that the bombardments would stir up anger in the population and that their wrath would be directed at the landed troops, the Normans welcomed their liberators with open arms, in spite of the ruin and the mourning.

The inhabitants of the liberated towns and villages proved themselves impervious to Vichy and German propaganda, which bemoaned the destruction, the better to vilify the Allies, and grateful to those men who had been prepared to lose their lives to bring the taste and colour of freedom back into their daily lives.

After the battle, civilians and soldiers shared the joys of liberation. While the former discovered the pleasures of Coca-Cola and chewing gum, the latter rapidly developed a taste for cider and calvados.

A blow-by-blow account of the Battle of Normandy

6th June
The beginning of the air and sea operations in Normandy. In 24 hours, the Allies landed 156,000 men (73,000 Americans, 83,000 British and Canadians) and 20,000 vehicles of all types. Their air forces made 11,000 sorties.

7th June
Liberation of Bayeux.

The arrival of the first convoy of the Phoenix elements off Arromanches; start of the construction of the artificial port.

8th June
Liberation of Port-en-Bessin.

9th June
Opening of an air-field by the Allies, in Saint-Laurent and Saint-Pierre du Mont.

10th June
Liberation of Isigny-sur-Mer.
The British reached Tilly-sur-Seulles; the Americans entered Balleroy.

11th June
The British 7th Armour took Tilly-sur-Seulles, but the Germans recaptured the village the same day.

12th June
Liberation of Carentan.
Winston Churchill and General Eisenhower spent a few hours in Normandy visiting the front.

13th June
In Caen, after the night's violent bombardments, most areas of the town were in flames.
East of the Orne, failure of the British 6th Airborne's counter attack.
A column of the British 7th Armour, heading for Caen, was repelled by the Germans at Villers-Bocage.
Liberation of Balleroy by the Americans.
General Bradley chose not to attack Saint-Lô, preferring to regroup his forces for the assault on Cherbourg.

14th June
The British 50th Infantry suspended their advance on Caen.
General de Gaulle spent the afternoon in Normandy. He met Montgomery, then went to Bayeux, where he established a Commissioner of the Republic, then visited Grandcamp and Isigny.

15th June
Liberation of Quinéville in the eastern Cotentin.

16th June
King George VI arrived in Normandy to visit General Montgomery.

17th June
The Allies had now landed 557,000 men and 81,000 vehicles.

18th June
Liberation of Barneville and Portbail, in the western Cotentin.

19th-21st June
Violent storm on the Seine Bay coast.
The artificial ports at Saint-Laurent-sur-Mer and Arromanches were seriously damaged.

20th June
Liberation of Valognes.

23rd June
The American 9th, 79th, and 4th Infantries reached the outskirts of Cherbourg, where the Germans totally destroyed the harbour and the port facilities.
Two thirds of the German tanks stationed in France were by now concentrated in Normandy. The 9th and 10th Panzer came from the Eastern Front.

24th June
Liberation of Caumont l'Eventé.

26th-30th June
The British started Operation Epsom south-west of Caen.
Liberation of Saint-Manvieu and Cheux.

27th June
Liberation of Cherbourg. Beginning of the reconstruction of the port facilities sabotaged by the Germans.

28th June
Suicide of General Dollman, commander of the German 7th Army.

30th June
The Allies had by now landed 875,000 men, 148,000 vehicles, 570,000 tonnes of munitions, merchandise and materials. Their air forces had made 163,000 sorties, eleven times more than the Luftwaffe.

2nd July
Marshal von Kluge replaced Marshal von Rundstedt as commander-in-chief of the German troops on the Western Front.

4ᵗʰ July
American Independence Day.
General Eisenhower inspected the
Normandy Front to celebrate this
168ᵗʰ Anniversary of the Declaration
of Independence, and lunched with
General Bradley near the Haye-
du-Puits.
The Allies had landed their millionth
soldier, 183,500 vehicles, and 650,000
tonnes of material and equipment.

7ᵗʰ July
The Canadians took control
of Carpiquet Airport.

8ᵗʰ July
Launch of Operation Goodwood
north of Caen.

9ᵗʰ July
The British and Canadians captured
the part of Caen on the left bank
of the Orne.

10ᵗʰ July
The divisions of the 1ˢᵗ US Army
headed for Saint-Lô and Coutances.

14ᵗʰ July
The liberated towns and villages
celebrated Bastille Day, despite
the mourning and the ruination.

16ᵗʰ July
The first freighter docked
in Cherbourg.

17ᵗʰ July
Field-Marshal Rommel, who had been
seriously wounded in an automobile
accident during an air raid near Livarot,
left Normandy for Germany.

18ᵗʰ-21ˢᵗ July
Operation Goodwood, east of Caen.

19ᵗʰ July
Complete liberation of Caen
and Saint-Lô.

22ⁿᵈ July
Winston Churchill visited
the Normandy front. In Caen,
he opened two Bailey bridges over
the Orne, respectively baptised
'Winston' and 'Churchill'.

25ᵗʰ July
Beginning of Operation Cobra
south-west of Saint-Lô

26ᵗʰ July
Start of Operation Spring south
of Caen.

27ᵗʰ July
By transferring three divisions from
the Pas-de-Calais to Normandy, Hitler
satisfied the requests of Marshal von
Kluge, who was desperately trying
to contain American progress in the
Cotentin.

28ᵗʰ July
The German Army began yielding
everywhere in Normandy.

29ᵗʰ July
Liberation of Coutances and Cérences

30ᵗʰ July
Montgomery launched Operation
Bluecoat.

31ˢᵗ July
Liberation of Avranches and Ducey
by the American 4ᵗʰ Armour, and
Granville by the 6ᵗʰ Armour. Most
of the troops then headed for Brittany.
The 15ᵗʰ Army Corps headed east,
towards Le Mans. Stationed mid-way
between Caen and Saint-Lô, the British
7ᵗʰ and 11ᵗʰ Armoured Divisions had
to prevent the German reinforcements
from reaching the Americans.
Arrival of the Polish 1ˢᵗ Armour
in Arromanches.

1ˢᵗ August.
Reorganisation of the Allied forces on
the Normandy front. General Patton took
command of the American 3ʳᵈ Army.

The Americans liberated Pontaubalut,
Pontorson, Percy.
The British liberated Bény-Bocage.
Arrival of the French 2ⁿᵈ Armoured
Division near Sainte-Marie-du-Mont.

2ⁿᵈ August
Liberation of Villedieu.

3ʳᵈ August
The American 1ˢᵗ Infantry took
Mortain.

4ᵗʰ August
Liberation of Villers-Bocage and Evrecy
by the British, who thus completed the
breakthrough in the hedgerow country.
The idea of surrounding the
7ᵗʰ German Army was becoming
clearer in Allied Staff Headquarters.

5ᵗʰ August
The British entered Aunay-sur-Odon;
the Americans liberated Saint-Pois
and Saint-Sever.

6th August

The British 43rd Division took Mont Pinçon.

7th August

German counter-attack in Mortain. Liberation of the ruins of Vire by the American 29th Infantry. General Eisenhower established his campaign HQ in Normandy, near Bayeux.

8th August

Engagement of the Canadians and Poles in Operation Totalize, south of Caen.

9th August

The German counter-offensive on Mortain was definitively thwarted. Liberation of Cauvaincourt and Saint-Sylvain by the Polish 1st Armour.

10th August

Liberation of Vimont by the British. The Canadians were 10 km from Falaise, but Montgomery interrupted Totalize, due to the heavy losses his troops had sustained.

11th August

The German forces in Normandy were surrounded in a 25 km pocket around Falaise.

12th August

Coming from Le Mans, the American 15th Army Corps (79th, 90th, 5th Armor and French 2nd Armour) entered Alençon, then headed for Argentan.

The German armies in Normandy began to retreat.

13th August

Liberation of Thury-Harcourt by the British 12th Army Corps.

14th August

Montgomery launched Operation Tractable to capture Falaise, with the Canadians and the Poles.

The French 2nd Armour and the American 5th Armour were making no headway at Argentan.

15th August.

The British 8th Army Corps and the 5th US Army Corps linked up north-west of Mortain.

The Polish 1st Armour held the bridgehead at Jort, on the Dives.

16th August

The Canadian 2nd Army Corps entered Falaise. The Canadian 4th Armour headed for Trun, capturing the bridge at Morteaux-Couliboeuf on the way.

17th August

Liberation of Falaise.

Two German divisions succeeded in escaping from the Falaise pocket, which was about to be closed by the Allies.

18th August

Marshal W. Model, who had replaced von Kluge as commander-in-chief of the German troops on the Western Front, ordered the German 5th and 7th Armies to retreat over the Touques.

Von Kluge, en route for Germany, wrote a letter to Hitler, then committed suicide.

Units from the Canadian 2nd Army Corps, the Polish 1st Armour and the 15th US Army Corps joined up near the villages of Saint-Lambert, Chambois and Mont-Ormel.

19th August

The Polish 1st Armoured Division and the American 90th Infantry closed the Falaise pocket at Chambois. Almost all the units of the German 7th Army were surrounded: 50,000 men were captured.

20th August

Complete liberation of Argentan.

General de Gaulle landed at, and visited, Maupertuis, near Cherbourg, Coutances and Avranches, before going on to Rennes.

21st August

The Canadian 4th Armour succeeded in connecting with the Poles of the Polish 1st Armour, who had been isolated on Mont-Ormel since the 19th; the Falaise Pocket was sealed tight.

The British 11th Armour reached the Touques and liberated L'Aigle. The Canadian 2nd Army Corps headed for Rouen. General de Gaulle met Eisenhower in his HQ in Tournières (Calvados), where he asked him to send Leclerc's men to Paris.

Photographic crédits

CANADIAN NATIONAL ARCHIVES / THE MEMORIAL, Caen: Front cover, pp. 22 bl, 50, 79 t, 80, 106 r, 107 r, 144, 147 tl, 147 br, 156, 158, 179 r, 188.

BROMBERG / MAIRIE DE CAEN Collection: pp. 88-89.

Private collections / THE MEMORIAL, Caen: pp. 183, 185.

Private collections / MAIRIE DE CAEN: pp. 23 tr, 76, 95 bl, 95 br, 115, 132 t, 139 tr, 142, 148 l, 148 r, 149 t, 150, 149 bl, 161, 193 tr.

All rights reserved / THE MEMORIAL, Caen: pp. 14, 17, 44 t, 44 l, 90, 91, 95 tl, 97, 118, 119 t, 119 bl, 119 br, 120, 121, 143, 171, 191.

US ARMY **/ THE MEMORIAL, Caen:** pp. 12, 18 t, 20, 21, 26, 55 l, 55 r, 59, 63, 66 t, 66 b, 67, 68, 70, 71, 74, 76, 77, 87, 95 tr, 100, 101, 102 r, 102 l, 104, 105, 106 r, 110, 122, 126, 131, 132 b, 134, 135, 137, 138 br, 139 bl, 160, 161, 167, 168, 174, 194 t, 194 b, 195.

BUNDESARCHIV, **Koblenz:** pp. 11, 30, 32, 33, 34l, 35 t, 36, 38, 39, 40, 41, 43, 45, 46, 47, 65, 93, 97, 113, 124, 166, 175.

DITE, Paris: pp. 116, 117, 150, 164, 165, 167, 192.

ECPAd, Paris: pp. 34 r, 35 b, 43, 98, 99, 107 l, 123, 125, 151, 162, 169, 173, 180, 181, 182.

IMPERIAL WAR MUSEUM, **London:** pp. 10, 15, 18 bl, 19, 22 tl, 22 tr, 22 br, 23 tl, 23 t centre, 23 b, 24, 25, 28, 29, 51, 52, 53, 57, 60, 72, 73, 78, 79 b, 81, 82, 83, 84, 85, 86, 96, 103, 112t, 112 b, 130, 140, 145, 149, 155, 159, 170, 187, 189, 193 br, back cover.

POLISH INSTITUTE / GENERAL SIKORSKY MUSEUM, London: p. 177.

MUSEE DE LA MARINE, Paris: p. 111.

MUSEE MEMORIAL MARECHAL LECLERC ET DE LA LIBERATION DE PARIS. MUSEE JEAN MOULIN, Paris: p. 168.

ROBERT CAPA R/MAGNUM PHOTOS: end-paper.

Art and Graphics: Alain Gouessant
Typographic design: Pascale Comte
Photoengraving: Atelier André Michel
Printed in February 2002 by Jombard, Evreux
ISBN: 2-914230-33-8
Dépôt légal : February 2002